BIG-CITY BAGS

BIG-CITY BAGS

Sew Handbags with Style, Sass, and Sophistication

Sara Lawson

Dedication

*To my wonderful husband, love of my life, Danny, and my awesome and fun-to-be-with
children, William and Violet. They love me exactly how I am, sewing and all.*

Big-City Bags:
Sew Handbags with Style, Sass, and Sophistication
© 2013 by Sara Lawson

Martingale®
19021 120th Ave. NE, Ste. 102
Bothell, WA 98011-9511 USA
ShopMartingale.com

Printed in China
18 17 16 15 14 13   8 7 6 5 4 3 2 1

Library of Congress Cataloging-in-Publication Data
is available upon request.

ISBN: 978-1-60468-293-9

MISSION STATEMENT

Dedicated to providing quality products and
service to inspire creativity.

Credits

President and CEO: Tom Wierzbicki
Editor in Chief: Mary V. Green
Design Director: Paula Schlosser
Managing Editor: Karen Costello Soltys
Acquisitions Editor: Karen M. Burns
Technical Editor: Rebecca Kemp Brent
Copy Editor: Melissa Bryan
Production Manager: Regina Girard
Cover and Interior Designer: Adrienne Smitke
Photographer: Brent Kane
Illustrator: Christine Erikson

CONTENTS

7 Introduction

8 Interfacing for Bags

12 Bag-Making Techniques

PROJECTS

21 Fireside Bowl Bag

27 Go-Go Bag

33 Meringue Clutch

39 Wonderland Bag

45 Bee Sweet Bag

51 Oh Spit! Diaper Bag

59 Lucky Denver Mint Bag

65 Chandelier Swing Bag

69 Miss Independent Bag

79 Honeymooner Suitcase

83 Piccadilly Circus Bag

89 Sound Check Bag

94 Resources

95 Acknowledgments

96 About the Author

INTRODUCTION

I am so intrigued by sewing. I love thinking about sewing-pattern instructions, shopping online for fabric, and devising new ways to finish projects. To me, sewing is like solving a puzzle, and all the different fabrics and techniques are pieces of that puzzle. There are always different ways to put the pieces together, but I challenge myself to come up with combinations that make each sewn item stunning and unique.

I began writing bag-sewing patterns late in 2011, when I should have been finishing up my handmade holiday gifts instead. I got a phone call from Pellon, an interfacing manufacturer, one day while I was Christmas shopping at the mall with my husband; the company was interested in a bag pattern for its Pellon Projects website. I told the rep that I would see about something after the New Year . . . and then I sent my Caliti Clutch sewing pattern to them about a week later.

Since then, my life has been a whirlwind of more and more bags. Between this book and the free patterns on my blog, I wrote 26 bag-sewing patterns in less than 10 months. It doesn't feel like that many at all! It has been an absolute joy, and I am learning so much with each bag I make. Words can't describe how wonderful it feels to be doing not only what I truly love, but also something that has the potential to spark creativity in others.

I have not used a store-bought bag in years. I truly believe that handmade bags don't necessarily have to *look* handmade. I think I've taken on the term "bag lady" full force with this book, making it my personal mission to turn around the stigma surrounding those two words. Handmade bags should be stylish. They should be hip. They should be fantastic and bold. And if they happen to be mistaken for store-bought bags, that's a bonus!

The 12 projects here are all intermediate- to advanced-level patterns. The Internet is such a great resource for so many free sewing patterns that I did not feel the need to start with an easy pouch or tote bag, because you can find all those types of goodies online. The illustrations and instructions for each of my patterns are designed to provide a great foundation and get you on the way to your new bag in no time. I am so honored that you are holding this book in your hands right now, and I can't wait to see what you create!

I hope you will take the patterns in this book and make them your own. Nothing makes me more excited than when a reader sends me an e-mail saying, "I made your bag pattern and I love it! I changed the flap a bit and added a longer strap, and it's just perfect for me!"

~Sara

INTERFACING FOR BAGS

One of my favorite topics is interfacing; you really cannot make a bag without it. Interfacing makes up 25% of my fabric stash . . . no lie! It's one of those things that you just need to have on hand at all times, because you'll use it in almost every project.

I use Pellon interfacing. If you live in a country where Pellon is not available, you may have luck finding the European brand Vilene, which is a fine alternative for making bags. Refer to the interfacing conversion chart below (which I put together with help from the lovely folks at Pellon).

INTERFACING CONVERSIONS	
PELLON	VILENE
Fusible Fleece (987F; green label)	Iron-On Lightweight Fleece (H630)
Fusible Thermolam Plus (TP971F; green label)	Iron-On High-Loft Fleece (H640) or Thermolam Plus (272)
Shape-Flex (SF 101; pink label)	Woven Fusible (G700)
Deco-Fuse (520)	Firm Interlining (S520)
Peltex Sew-In Ultra Firm Stabilizer (70; yellow label)	Heavy Sew-In (S80)
Peltex One-Sided Fusible (71F)	Firm Iron-On (S520)
Décor Bond (809)	Iron-On (H250)

Most of my favorite interfacings are fusible. When fusing interfacing to your fabric, you should always use a pressing cloth. This will protect the fabric from excessive heat, while also keeping the adhesive from the interfacing off your iron. Always place the bumpy or tacky side of the interfacing against the wrong side of the fabric.

Needed Know-How

Whenever you're fusing interfacing to fabric, follow the manufacturer's instructions carefully for product-specific guidelines.

Fusible Fleece (Pellon 987F)

You can purchase fusible fleece by the yard at your local fabric store. It is fusible on one side, which means you can feel the "glue" on one surface, and this is the side to position against the wrong side of your fabric. This interfacing has a bit of loft. I like using it, but I usually reserve it for a very specific purpose, such as to add extra body to the lining of a bag, to create padded straps without extra bulk, or to make small flaps. I don't often use it for the bag exterior, because I have found that its loft can make the fabric look crinkly when used over a large area.

One way to smooth your fabric when using fusible fleece is by first fusing a layer of Shape-Flex (discussed on page 10) to the fabric, and then following it with a layer of fusible fleece.

Another great use for fusible fleece is to reinforce magnetic snaps. Every time you open and close a magnetic snap, it puts pressure on the fabric. To resist everyday wear and tear, slide the snap prongs through the fabric and a small square of fleece before closing the prongs. With this reinforcement, you needn't worry about the fabric tearing under the strain of the magnetic snap. ①

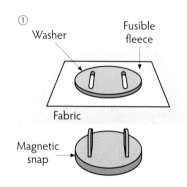

Fusible Thermolam Plus (Pellon TP971F)

I absolutely love Thermolam Plus, a needled fleece that is denser and flatter than generic fusible fleece. When I'm making a bag or other accessory, I like it to have body; even for a simple tote bag, just two layers of fabric is too thin for me. This is a matter of personal preference, but I want my bags to have some substance and be able to carry 20 pounds without tearing at the bottom. So I use Thermolam Plus fused to the bag's exterior fabric, sometimes in combination with either Shape-Flex or fusible fleece fused to the bag's lining fabric.

Thermolam Plus, once fused, leaves the fabric looking nice and smooth. Test a small piece on your exterior fabric; depending on your iron, you may need to apply heat longer than the manufacturer recommends, but be careful not to damage the fabric. Sometimes I leave the iron in place up to double the recommended time.

Finely Fused

I like to press Thermolam Plus with the fabric right side up on top of the fleece, using a mist of water on the fabric. When I'm sure it's properly fused, I flip the layers over and press again on top of the interfacing. This leaves the fabric incredibly flat and smooth.

Shape-Flex (Pellon SF101)

I use Shape-Flex, a fusible woven interfacing, in all of my bags. It is the most important interfacing in my stash, and I rely on it for a variety of uses. I fuse woven interfacing to every pocket I make, and I use it to reinforce the area around a zipper.

Once fused, Shape-Flex gives quilting-weight cotton the sturdy feel of a home-decor or canvas-weight fabric. As with the interfacings already discussed, the rough, tacky side should go against the fabric's wrong side for fusing. Shape-Flex is perfect as a stand-alone interfacing in a pouch or other small project, or you can combine it with other interfacings.

Deco-Fuse (Pellon 520)

I love this interfacing; it's wonderful in so many ways and perfect for making a very stiff bag.

Deco-Fuse is a great way to give your bags a store-bought look, because it always leaves the fabric nice and smooth after fusing, never with a puckered, fused look. It holds finger-pressing nicely, so sometimes I don't bother pressing the seams with an iron.

Even though Deco-Fuse is very stiff, it's only as thick as a piece of construction paper, which makes it reasonably easy to sew. However, as with any stiff interfacing, maneuvering your bag through the sewing machine can be tricky. Sew slowly, and be creative; for instance, you may sew from one edge to the center of a line of stitching, stop to reposition the bag, and sew the second half of the seam from the other edge to the center. Honestly, no one is going to see the wrong side of your bag, so it doesn't have to be the prettiest stitching in the world. You may also find it easier to use binder clips instead of pins for holding the layers of fabric and interfacing in place.

Peltex Sew-In (Pellon 70)

This stiff interfacing is a little thicker than Deco-Fuse. Because it is a Sew-In interfacing, it will not fuse to your fabric. You can baste the interfacing to the fabric ⅛" inside the seam allowance, but I prefer this alternate method: Cut one piece each of Shape-Flex and Peltex Sew-In the same size as the pattern piece. Trim ½" from the edges of the Peltex Sew-In. Center the Peltex Sew-In on the wrong side of the fabric, and then place the Shape-Flex on top with its fusible side down. When you fuse the Shape-Flex, it will seal the Peltex Sew-In to the fabric along the ½" edges. Using a smaller piece of Peltex Sew-In also reduces the bulk of the seam allowance.

Bag-handle inserts are another great reason to have some Peltex Sew-In around. Some sewing patterns for bags instruct you to create a double-folded piece for each handle so that the raw edges are not exposed. When using this technique, I cut a narrow strip of Peltex Sew-In for each handle and slide the interfacing into the prepared handle pieces before topstitching the long edges. It makes the handles very stable. Fusible fleece and Thermolam Plus can also be used as handle inserts depending on the look desired.

While I prefer to use Deco-Fuse in my bags, Peltex Sew-In can be a great substitution.

Peltex One–Sided Fusible (Pellon 71F)

Before the release of Deco-Fuse, I used Peltex One-Sided Fusible interfacing all the time, but it has taken a backseat in my stash. It's great when you want to interface a small area of a project (such as the flap of a bag or clutch), but I find that sometimes it leaves large areas such as the exterior of a bag with a fused or crinkly look.

Peltex One-Sided Fusible is a stiff interfacing like Peltex Sew-In and Deco-Fuse. If you prefer stiffness and fusibility, choose the One-Sided Fusible rather than Deco-Fuse.

Décor Bond (Pellon 809)

This interfacing often pops up in my bags. If there are bag panels or handles that need to look stiff without crinkling at folds and creases, this is the interfacing for you.

My favorite application of this interfacing is to use it in two layers. First, I fuse a layer of Shape-Flex against the wrong side of my fabric, and then I add two layers of Décor Bond, cutting the Décor Bond ½" smaller on all its edges to keep bulk out of the seam allowances.

One or two layers of Décor Bond will help a bag stand up by itself, but without quite as much stiffness as you'll get with Deco-Fuse, Peltex Sew-In, or Peltex One-Sided Fusible..

It's a Wonder

If you don't have interfacing handy, Pellon Wonder Under (a fusible web) will turn any fabric into a fusible interfacing. For example, you can use fusible web to fuse a piece of canvas or batting to your quilting cotton, adding lots of body.

There are no hard-and-fast rules for using interfacing. I suggest that the best way to learn more about interfacing is to use it in all of your projects. Tweak your interfacing choice based on your personal preference: what kind of shape are you interested in, how much stiffness, what kind of body? There are unlimited possibilities!

BAG-MAKING TECHNIQUES

This section explains several different methods for installing zippers, as well as how to use a variety of purse hardware and how to attach leather handles to a bag by hand. Each technique appears in at least one bag in this book, and knowing how to add these special touches will enable you to give a completely individualized look to any bag you sew.

Top Zip

This is, in my opinion, one of the easiest zipper applications. It is most commonly used in simple zipped pouches. Use fabric scraps to make zipper tabs so that your zipper will begin and end neatly at the top of your bag.

1. Press two 1½" x 3" fabric scraps in half, wrong sides together, matching the short edges. Open the fabric and fold the short edges to the center so that they meet at the crease. Refold along the original crease and press once more. You have created two tiny pieces of double-fold tape. ①

2. Trim the zipper tape so that it is exactly 1" shorter than the edge where you're inserting it. Do not cut off the zipper pull or the zipper's upper stops. Slide one end of the zipper into a prepared double-fold tape, with the end of the zipper touching the center crease, and pin. Edgestitch the fabric ⅛" from the double folds and zipper, taking care to catch both folds in the seam. Repeat for the other end of the zipper and the remaining piece of double-fold tape.

3. Trim the excess double-fold tape on both sides of the zipper so that it is the same width as the zipper tape. ②

4. Align the prepared zipper on one bag exterior piece, right sides together, positioning the zipper ends ½" from the bag side edges. Pin in place. With a zipper foot and ¼" seam allowance, stitch the zipper in place, including both zipper tabs. Do not sew into the ½" areas beyond the zipper ends. ③

5. Place the lining front on the bag front and zipper, right sides together, and pin in place. Sew directly on top of the previous stitches.

6. Turn the fabrics right side out and press. Edgestitch the zipper edges, ⅛" from the zipper tape.

7. Repeat steps 4–6 for the other side of the zipper. Remove the zipper foot from your machine. ④

8. Follow the specific pattern instructions to continue construction of the bag. Usually, you will sew the bag pieces, right sides together, and the lining pieces, right sides together, along the three unfinished edges.

Zipper Panel

This method for inserting a zipper is often used in a three-dimensional (rather than flat) bag, where the bag exterior and lining are assembled independently before being attached along the zipper in the last step. A bit of hand sewing is involved in this method. These instructions are for a zipper that is centered along the zipper panel.

1. Cut the bag's zipper panel in half lengthwise.

2. Lay the two pieces right sides together along the newly cut edge. With a fabric marker, mark 1" from each short end. Sew from each mark to the nearest edge, using a ⅝" seam allowance, backstitching at each end of the seams. Each line of stitching will be only 1" long.

3. Set your machine for a basting stitch. Using a ⅝" seam allowance, baste between the two lines of stitching from the previous step. Press open the seam allowances along the entire seam. ⑤

4. Place the zipper on top of the basted zipper panel, with wrong sides up and the zipper teeth on top of the basting stitches. Pin in place.

5. Using a zipper foot, sew all around the zipper, ¼" from the zipper teeth. ⑥

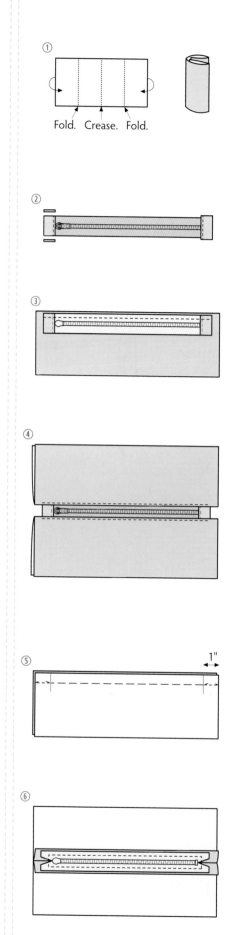

① Fold. Crease. Fold.

⑤ 1"

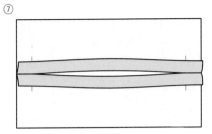

6. With the right side of the bag's zipper panel facing you, use a seam ripper to remove the basting stitches.

7. Repeat steps 1 and 2 to prepare the lining's zipper panel. Press the seam allowances to the wrong side between the short end seams rather than basting. ⑦

Zippered Pocket

I have learned two different ways of installing a zippered pocket. The first method (which I used for the first zipper I ever installed!) encloses all the zipper's raw edges. Although this sounds nice, this method makes it a bit tricky to achieve a neat right-side appearance. In the second method, the bag and lining are sewn with right sides together, but the zipper edges are visible when you open the pocket. Choose the method that suits you best.

METHOD 1

1. Draw a rectangle on the wrong side of the bag piece where the pocket will go, at least 2" below the top edge of the fabric. The rectangle should be ½" wide and ½" shorter than the zipper, and centered on the bag piece. Draw a line down the center of the rectangle, beginning and ending ¼" from the rectangle's short ends. Draw a V at each end, connecting the centerline to the rectangle's corners. ⑧

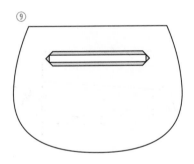

2. Cut along the centerline and the Vs. Press the raw edges to the wrong side along the original rectangle. ⑨

> **Simple Slicing**
> *I like to use my seam ripper to start the opening before finishing the cut with my scissors.*

3. Cut the pocket piece as directed in the project instructions, usually double the height of the finished pocket. Place the zipper on the pocket fabric, right sides up, with one edge of the zipper along the lower edge of the pocket.

4. Place the pressed opening in the bag fabric directly over the zipper, with the majority of the pocket fabric lying up and away from the zipper opening. Pin all the layers in place. Edgestitch ⅛" from the pressed edge along the bottom of the opening only. ⑩

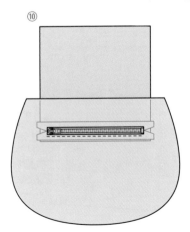

5. Press the pocket fabric away from the zipper, toward the bottom of the bag. Turn the unit over so that the wrong side of the bag fabric is facing you. Fold the pocket, right sides together, matching the raw edge to the free edge of the zipper. Hold the pocket and zipper in place with your fingers. ⑪

6. Flip the unit back over so that the right side of the bag fabric is facing you. Pin the top zipper tape and pocket in place. Edgestitch the top and sides of the opening, connecting with the previous edge stitches and keeping the lower part of the pocket out of the way.

7. Flip the unit back to the wrong side. Match the pocket fabric raw edges and sew the two side seams, folding the bag fabric out of the way.

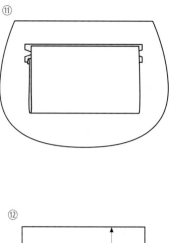

METHOD 2

1. Cut the pocket piece as directed in the project instructions, usually double the height of the finished pocket. On the wrong side of the pocket, measure and mark a horizontal line that is halfway, plus ½", from the pocket's upper edge. Draw a second horizontal line ½" below the first.

2. Draw vertical lines 1" from each side of the pocket piece, connecting the horizontal lines. The result is a rectangular box.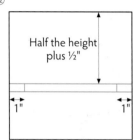

3. Draw a rectangle on the right side of the bag piece where the pocket will go. Place the marked pocket on the bag piece, right sides together, with the placement marks aligned. The pocket should be at least 1" above the bottom raw edge of the fabric and at least ¾" from the bag's side edges. Pin in place and then sew along the drawn lines to make a rectangular box.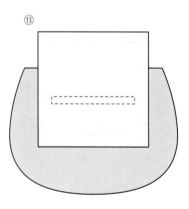

4. Draw a line down the center of the rectangle, beginning and ending ¼" from the rectangle's short ends. Draw a V at each end, connecting the centerline to the rectangle's corners. Cut along the lines, taking care not to cut into the stitching. (See "Simple Slicing" on page 14.)

5. Turn the pocket to the wrong side of the bag, through the opening, and press.

6. With right sides up, center the zipper underneath the opening and pin in place. Make sure that the pocket is lying flat and away from the opening. Edgestitch around the opening, ⅛" from the pressed fabric edges.

7. Fold the pocket in half just above the zipper, right sides together. Sew along the side and bottom edges using a ½" seam allowance.

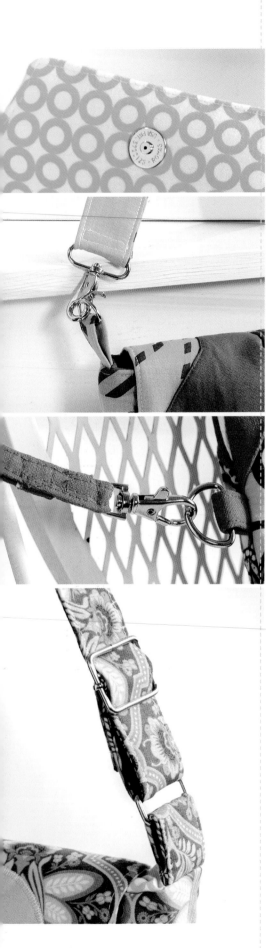

Magnetic Snaps

Magnetic snaps are the most common type of purse hardware, and they are very simple to install. I use magnetic snaps on any bag that is not closed with a flap or zipper. The parts of the snap closure are usually inserted into opposite sides of the bag lining, or into the wrong side of a flap and the right side of the bag panel underneath the flap.

1. Prepare the bag fabric with interfacing. Also cut two 2" squares of Thermolam Plus or fusible fleece to reinforce the bag fabric for regular use.

2. With a fabric marker or chalk, mark prong placements 1½" from the top of the bag or 1½" from the lower edge of the flap. Also mark prong placements at the centers of the reinforcement squares. If the snap set includes washers, use one as a stencil for the placement markings; if not, use the thinner half of the snap (with the raised center) as a guide. Cut a small slit at each mark.

Sealed for Security

I like to put a dab of seam sealant on the slits cut in bag and lining fabrics before proceeding with the snap installation.

3. Slide the prongs of the snap through the slits from the right side of the fabric. Place the Thermolam Plus, then the washer (if included with the snap), over the prongs. Fold the prongs outward, making sure they lie flat against the bag fabric and reinforcement. (See the illustration on page 9.)

4. Repeat the process to insert the other half of the magnetic snap.

Purse Feet

Purse feet are inexpensive and easy to install. You can add them to any bag with a bottom. It is easiest to insert the purse feet into the bottom piece of the bag before bag assembly.

1. With a fabric marker, draw lines on the wrong side of the prepared bag bottom, 1½" from each edge. Also cut four 2" squares of Thermolam Plus or fusible fleece to reinforce the bag fabric, one for each foot location.

2. Make a small slit at each of the four corners where the lines intersect. I recommend reinforcing the slits in the fabric with a small dab of seam sealant.

3. Slide one metal purse foot through a slit from the right side of the fabric.

4. To reinforce the fabric, cut a slit in the center of a piece of fusible fleece or Thermolam Plus for each foot and slide it onto the prong, against the wrong side of the fabric. Open the prongs outward.

5. Repeat the process to insert the remaining feet.

Metal D-Rings, O-Rings, and Swivel Clips

These bits of purse hardware are available in a variety of sizes, and they all involve the same technique for attaching straps to a bag or clutch.

1. Assemble the handle or strap as directed in the project instructions.

2. Press ½" to the wrong side on each end of the handle. Press an additional 1" to the wrong side on each end, or as otherwise directed for your project.

3. Slide one end of the handle through the hardware so that the ring lies in the second crease on the handle. Sew a small rectangle near the first fold, enclosing the raw edges and securing the hardware. Repeat for the other end of the handle. ⑭

Metal Slider for an Adjustable Strap

This hardware, which makes any purse strap adjustable, really is invaluable. One minute your bag tucks neatly under your arm, and the next it becomes a cross-body bag. This technique requires a sewn strap piece, another piece (the strap extender) that is the same width as the strap and at least 4" long, and the slider plus a rectangular ring. ⑮

1. Construct the strap and strap extender as instructed for the specific project, enclosing all the long raw edges.

2. Slide the rectangular ring to the middle of the strap extender. Fold the extender in half around the ring, matching the raw edges, and position it on one side of the bag's upper edge. Baste the layers together ¼" from the raw edges.

3. Baste one end of the strap to the side of the bag opposite the strap extender. Weave the free end of the strap through the slider, passing over and under the center bar. Pass the strap end through the rectangular ring from right side to wrong side. ⑯

4. Press ½" to the wrong side on the free end of the strap, and then press an additional 1" to the wrong side. Wrap the strap end around the slider's center bar, underneath the previously woven strap, so that the bar rests in the second pressed fold. Be sure the strap is not twisted. Sew a small rectangle through the strap end near the first fold, enclosing the first pressed edges and securing the hardware. ⑰

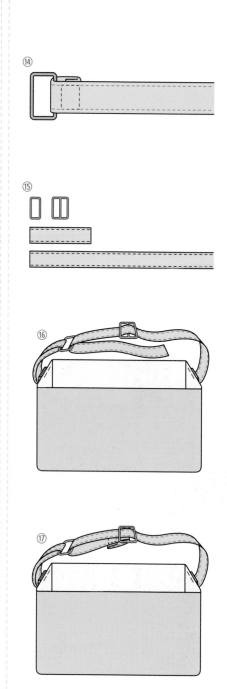

Twist Locks

I often see twist locks on store-bought bags and clutches, so why not add one to something you've made yourself? With a little glue and a bit of patience, you can add a twist lock to any bag with a flap. These instructions are for inserting one type of twist lock; always refer to the manufacturer's instructions for the hardware you choose.

1. Assemble the bag flap and then mark a dot on the flap exterior, centered 1" above the lower edge. Center the oval frame of the twist lock over the dot and draw around the center of the oval. Cut along the traced oval. Test the oval lock to be sure it fits snugly inside the hole; if the opening is too large the lock will fall out, so a snug fit is essential (otherwise you'll have to remake the flap). Apply a small amount of fabric glue inside the ridge of the oval frame and adhere it to the fabric, applying gentle pressure for several minutes. Some twist locks have prongs at the back of the frame; if this is the case, insert the prongs through the flap and then flatten them.

A twist lock and its component parts

Stick to It

I recommend UHU or Gutterman fabric glue for installing twist locks.

2. Mark a dot on the bag front, centered under the location of the lock frame when the flap is closed. Center the twist lock over the dot and draw two lines to mark the prong placements. Cut a small slit through the fabric along each line and apply seam sealant to the slits. Repeat the process to draw and cut two slits at the center of a 2" x 2" square of Thermolam Plus.

3. Insert the prongs of the locking piece through the slits from the bag's right side. Slide the piece of Thermolam Plus onto the prongs, followed by the washer (if included with the twist lock). Open the prongs outward to lie against the bag wrong side.

Leather Handles

Purse handles come in many sizes, colors, and thicknesses. A good strap length for a shoulder bag is 24" to 28", while handles at least 15" long work well for handbags. Many handles even come with prepunched tabs, allowing a hand-sewing needle to pass easily through the leather tabs. Here's an easy way to attach those handles that will also keep them firmly attached to your bag.

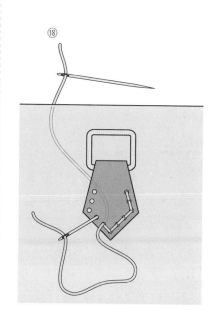

1. Begin with two strong hand-sewing needles and two 18" lengths of thread. Use a heavy-duty thread (upholstery, tapestry, or nylon) or a double (or even triple) strand of regular sewing-machine thread. Thread each needle and knot the ends.

2. Measure and mark the handle tab placements on the bag. It may be easier to attach the handles to a bag front or back prepared with interfacing before assembling the bag.

3. Place one handle tab at the corresponding mark. Beginning with the prepunched hole at one upper corner of the tab, insert one needle through the tab and fabric from the right side. Give the thread a firm tug to hide the knot inside the hole. Bring the second needle through the same hole from the wrong side, through the fabric first and then the tab.

4. Take the needles through the second hole in opposite directions and pull tight. Repeat for the third and successive holes, working around the tab to the other upper corner. The result is a solid line of stitches on both the right and wrong sides, although each needle is actually making a simple running stitch. Keep the tab held firmly against the fabric as you sew. ⑱

5. When you reach the opposite corner of the tab, stitch across the tab area through the bag fabric only so that the stitches are not visible on the finished bag. Tie off both thread ends securely. Repeat to attach the remaining handle tabs.

Sizing it Up
Bag dimensions throughout the book are listed as width x height x depth.

FIRESIDE BOWL BAG

FINISHED BAG: 14½" x 11" x 7"

This bag reminds me of going to the bowling alley in the summer: the worn bowling shoes, the smooth bowling ball, and the slick floor. Although the shape of this bag is familiar, your choice of fabrics will give it your own unique style!

Materials

Yardage is based on 42"-wide fabric.

⅝ yard of purple print for exterior

⅝ yard of green solid for accents and strap

1 fat quarter *or* ¼ yard of dark-gray solid for trim

1⅛ yards of teal print for lining

1 yard of Thermolam Plus fusible fleece

1 yard of Deco-Fuse fusible interfacing

1 yard of Shape-Flex fusible woven interfacing

1 zipper, 18" long

2 metal swivel clips (1½" opening)

2 metal D-rings (¾")

Cutting

The patterns for the accent piece and main panel are on pages 25 and 26.

From the purple print, cut:
2 main panels, *on fold,* for exterior front and back
1 rectangle, 7¼" x 18", for exterior zipper panel

From the green solid, cut:
1 rectangle, 4" x 30", for strap
2 accent pieces, *on fold*
1 rectangle, 8" x 25¾", for exterior bottom
2 rectangles, 3" x 4", for strap extenders

From the dark-gray solid, cut *on the bias:* *
2 strips, 1" x 18", for accent trim
2 strips, 1" x 8", for bottom trim

*Piece the strips as necessary if using a regular quarter-yard cut.

From the teal print, cut:
2 main panels, *on fold,* for lining front and back
1 rectangle, 7¼" x 18", for lining zipper panel
1 rectangle, 8" x 25¾", for lining bottom
2 rectangles, 9" x 16", for pockets

From the Thermolam Plus, cut:
4 main panels, *on fold,* for exterior and lining fronts and backs
2 rectangles, 7¼" x 18", for zipper panel
2 rectangles, 8" x 25¾", for exterior and lining bottoms

From the Deco-Fuse, cut:
2 main panels, *on fold;* trim ½" from all sides

From the Shape-Flex, cut:
2 rectangles, 9" x 16", for pockets
1 rectangle, 4" x 30", for strap
2 rectangles, 3" x 4", for strap extenders
2 accent pieces, *on fold*

Fuse the Fabrics and Interfacings

1. Fuse the appropriate pieces of Thermolam Plus to the wrong side of the exterior and lining main panels. Repeat with the exterior and lining zipper panels and bottoms.

2. Center a piece of Deco-Fuse on the interfaced side of one exterior main panel and fuse in place. Repeat with the second exterior main panel.

3. Fuse the Shape-Flex pieces to the wrong side of the corresponding fabric pieces for the strap, strap extenders, pockets, and accents.

Make the Zipper Panel

All seam allowances are ½" unless otherwise noted.

1. Cut the exterior zipper panel in half lengthwise to yield two 3⅝" x 18" pieces. Repeat with the lining zipper panel.

2. Insert the zipper and prepare the lining, following the instructions in "Zipper Panel" on page 13.

Make the Strap

1. Fold one strap extender in half, wrong sides together, to make a 1½" x 4" rectangle; press. Open the fold and press both long edges so that they meet at the center crease. Refold along the original crease and press once more, enclosing the raw edges, to make a ¾" x 4" double-folded strip. Edgestitch ⅛" from each long edge. Make two.

2. Construct the strap in the same way; the strap will finish 1" wide.

3. Fold one strap extender in half, matching the raw edges, and slide a metal D-ring into the crease. Make two.

4. Baste a prepared strap extender to each short end of the zipper panel, right sides together, centering the strap extender and matching the raw edges. ①

5. Press ½" to the wrong side on each short end of the prepared strap. Fold and press an additional 1" to the wrong side on each end.

6. Slide a swivel clip onto each end of the strap, nestling it into the second crease. Sew a small rectangle on each end, enclosing the first pressed edges and securing the swivel clip. ②

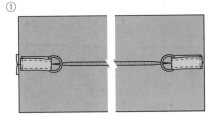

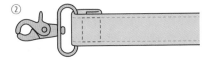

Assemble the Zipper and Bottom Panels

1. Fold the exterior bottom in half widthwise. Measure and mark 1" from each corner at the cut end. Draw a diagonal line connecting each mark with the corner of the fold at the corresponding side edge. Cut along the lines to taper the bag bottom. Discard the scraps, and open the tapered piece. ③

2. Fold the bottom trim strips in half lengthwise, wrong sides together, and press. Align the raw edge of a trim strip with one short end of the bag bottom, right sides together. Pin in place and then sew using a ¼" seam allowance. Trim the excess at the sides. Repeat for the remaining short end of the bag bottom. ④

3. Place the zipper panel and bag bottom right sides together, matching the short raw edges. Sew using a ⅜" seam allowance. Press the seam allowances toward the bag bottom, pressing the trim toward the zipper panel. Topstitch on the bag bottom, ⅛" from each seam. The joined panels create a ring. ⑤

4. Taper the lining bottom and join the lining bottom and zipper panels, right sides together, along their short ends in the same way, omitting the trim.

Assemble the Exterior

1. Fold the accent trim strips in half lengthwise, wrong sides together, and press. Place a trim strip along the upper edge of an accent piece, aligning the raw edges, and pin in place. Sew using a ⅜" seam allowance. Trim the excess at the sides. Press the seam allowances toward the accent piece, pressing the trim in the opposite direction. Repeat to prepare the second accent piece.

2. Position one accent piece on the right side of the exterior front, matching the side and bottom raw edges. Topstitch on the accent piece, ⅛" below the trim, to attach the accent to the main panel. Continue stitching ⅛" from the raw edges all the way around the accent piece. ⑥

3. Repeat step 2 to attach the second accent piece to the exterior back.

4. Pin the exterior front to the assembled bottom/zipper panel, right sides together, matching the seam lines to the notches and easing as necessary. Sew around the entire bag front. Clip the seam allowances along the curves, being careful not to cut into the stitches.

5. Unzip the zipper. Repeat step 4 to attach the exterior back to the remaining raw edge of the bottom/zipper panel. Turn the bag right side out and press.

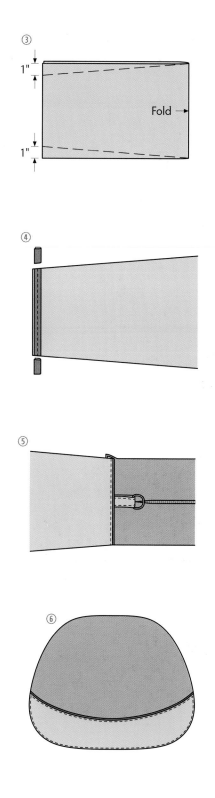

Make the Pockets

1. Fold one pocket in half widthwise, right sides together. Sew along the three raw edges, leaving a 3" opening along one edge for turning.

2. Trim the corners diagonally to reduce bulk. Turn the pocket right side out and press, turning the seam allowances to the wrong side along the opening.

3. Topstitch ⅛" from the folded edge, closing the opening as you sew. Make two.

Assemble the Lining

1. Finger-press one main-panel lining piece and one pocket in half to find their centers. Place the pocket on the lining piece, right sides up, aligning the center creases and positioning the bottom edge of the pocket (the edge opposite the fold) 2" above the bottom of the lining front. Pin in place.

2. Edgestitch the pocket sides and bottom to the lining, sewing ⅛" from the pocket edges and backstitching at the top of the pocket. The folded, topstitched edge remains open.

3. Repeat steps 1 and 2 to attach the second pocket to the second main-panel lining piece.

4. Place the assembled lining bottom/zipper panel and one lining pocket/main panel right sides together with the seam lines at the notches and pin, easing as necessary. Sew using a ⅝" seam allowance. Clip the seam allowances along the curves, being careful not to cut into the stitches.

5. Repeat step 4 to sew the remaining lining pocket/main panel to the remaining raw edge of the lining bottom/zipper panel. Press the seams.

Seams Great

Using a slightly wider seam allowance for the lining than the exterior will ensure a better fit in the finished bag.

A color variation of the Fireside Bowl Bag

Finish the Bag

1. Place the lining inside the bag exterior, wrong sides together. Slip-stitch the pressed edges of the lining opening to the wrong side of the zipper.

2. Use the swivel clips to attach each end of the strap to the metal D-rings.

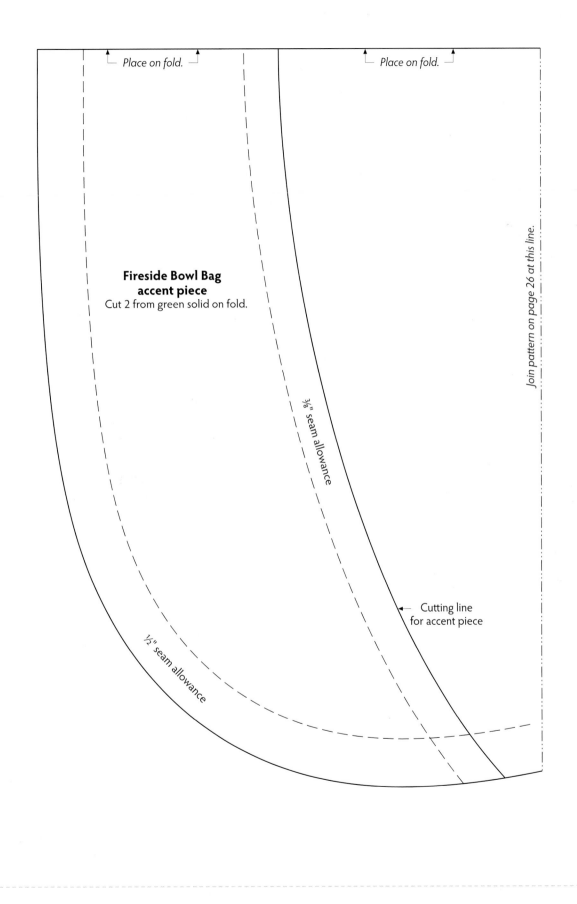

Place on fold.

Place on fold.

**Fireside Bowl Bag
accent piece**
Cut 2 from green solid on fold.

Join pattern on page 26 at this line.

⅜" seam allowance

Cutting line
for accent piece

½" seam allowance

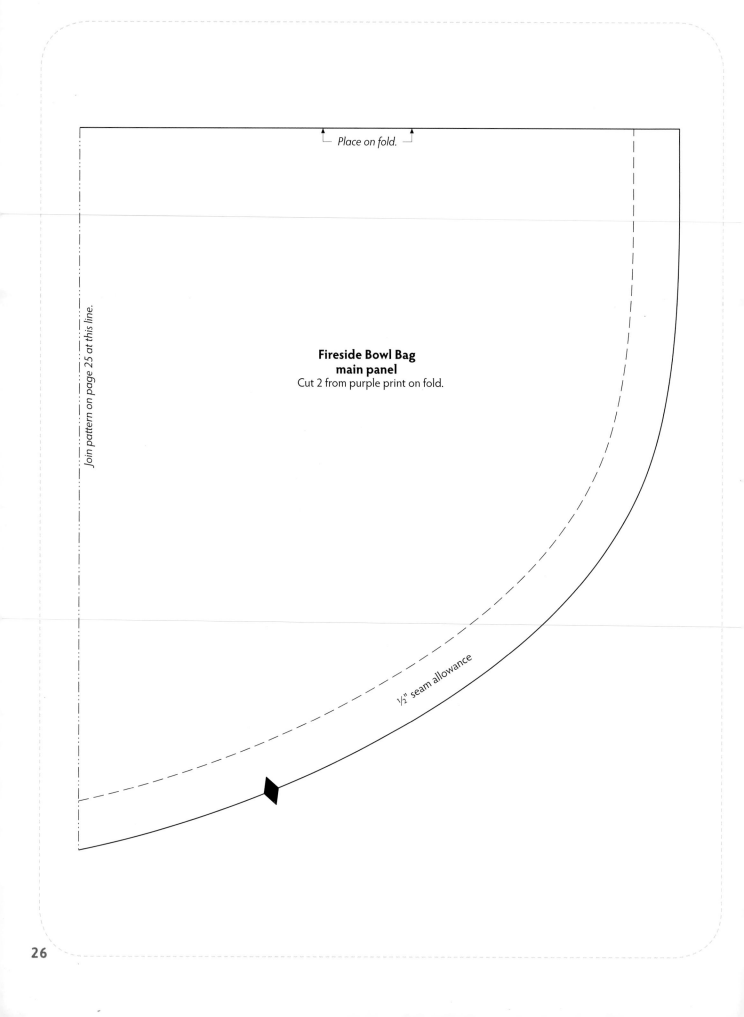

Place on fold.

Join pattern on page 25 at this line.

**Fireside Bowl Bag
main panel**
Cut 2 from purple print on fold.

½" seam allowance

GO-GO BAG

FINISHED BAG: 12" x 9"

This bag uses a metal twist lock, which might be a new bit of purse hardware for you to try. With the comfort of a messenger bag and the style of something more, you'll be proud to carry this bag and show off your favorite fabric. Despite its moderate size, this bag can hold a lot, making it perfect when you're on the go-go!

Materials

Yardage is based on 42"-wide fabric.

¾ yard of black print for exterior
1 yard of aqua solid for accent and lining
1 yard of Shape-Flex fusible woven interfacing
1 yard of Thermolam Plus fusible fleece
2 zippers, 9" long
2 metal swivel clips (1½" opening)
2 metal D-rings (¾")
1 metal twist lock
Seam sealant
Fabric glue

Cutting

The pattern for the accent piece is on page 32.

From the black print, cut:
1 rectangle, 4" x 24", for strap
2 rectangles, 11" x 14", for exterior front and back
1 rectangle, 8" x 12", for exterior flap
2 rectangles, 3" x 4", for strap extenders

From the aqua solid, cut:
2 rectangles, 11" x 14", for lining front and back
1 rectangle, 8" x 12", for lining flap
2 rectangles, 9" x 12", for pockets
2 rectangles, 4" x 10", for closure
1 accent piece, *on fold*

From the Shape-Flex, cut:
1 rectangle, 4" x 24", for strap
2 rectangles, 3" x 4", for strap extenders
2 rectangles, 9" x 12", for pockets
1 accent piece, *on fold*

From the Thermolam Plus, cut:
4 rectangles, 11" x 14", for exterior and lining fronts and backs
1 rectangle, 8" x 12", for exterior flap
1 rectangle, 7" x 11", for lining flap
2 rectangles, 3" x 9", for closure
1 square, 2" x 2", for reinforcement

Fuse the Fabrics and Interfacings

1. Fuse the Shape-Flex pieces to the wrong side of the corresponding fabric pieces for the strap, strap extenders, pockets, and accent.

2. Fuse the Thermolam Plus pieces to the wrong side of the corresponding pieces for the exterior front, back, and flap, and the lining front and back. Center pieces of Thermolam Plus on the lining flap and both closure rectangles and fuse.

Assemble the Flap

All seam allowances are ½" unless otherwise noted.

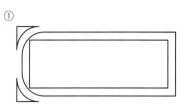

1. Lay a closure rectangle wrong side up, and trace a drinking glass or other round object at both corners of one short end. Place the closure rectangles right sides together and pin. Cut along the marked curves through all layers. ①

2. Sew along both long edges and the curved edge of the front closure piece. Clip the seam allowances along the curves, being careful not to cut into the stitches. Turn right side out and press. Edgestitch ⅛" from all the finished edges.

3. Repeat step 1 with the exterior and lining flap pieces.

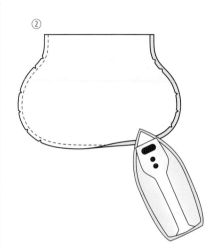

4. Stay stitch ¼" from the raw edges of the accent piece, leaving the short straight edge unsewn. Clip the seam allowance along the curves, cutting only halfway to the stitching. Press the raw edges to the wrong side along the stitches. ②

5. Finger-press the flap, accent piece, and front closure in half to mark the centers.

6. Place the accent piece on the exterior flap, right sides up, matching the centers and aligning the raw edges at the top of the flap. Pin generously.

7. Edgestitch the accent piece, sewing ⅛" from the pressed edge. ③

8. Place the exterior and lining flaps right sides together and sew, leaving the long straight edge open. Trim the seam allowances to ¼" and clip along the curves. Turn right side out and press.

9. Edgestitch ⅛" from the finished edges of the flap.

Install the Twist Lock

1. Mark the lock placement on the prepared closure, centered 1" above the curved end. Mark the location of the other half of the lock on the bag front, centered 7" below the upper edge.

2. Referring to "Twist Locks" on page 18, install the lock pieces in the closure and exterior front, using the 2" square of Thermolam Plus to reinforce the exterior front location.

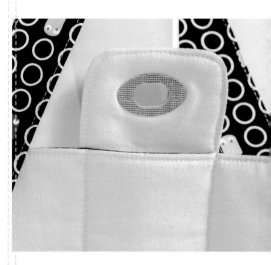

④

Stitch.

3. Place the closure on top of the completed flap, aligning the centers and placing the raw edge of the closure along the open upper edge of the flap. Pin in place; the closure will extend beyond the bottom of the flap.

4. Sew again on top of the closure's edgestitching to attach the closure to the flap. Stitch only along the edges that lie on top of the flap. ④

Make the Pockets

1. Draw a ½" x 8½" rectangle on the wrong side of the lining front, 3" below the upper edge and centered from side to side.

2. Refer to "Zippered Pocket" on page 14 to stitch the pocket into the lining front. The sample bag was created using method 1 for this step.

3. Attach the remaining pocket to the bag back (the exterior panel without the twist lock) in the same way.

Make the Strap

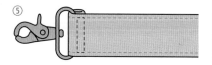

⑤

1. Fold one strap extender in half, wrong sides together, to make a 1½" x 4" rectangle; press. Open the fold and press both long edges to the wrong side so that they meet at the center crease. Refold along the original crease and press once more, enclosing the raw edges, to make a ¾" x 4" double-folded strip. Edgestitch ⅛" from each long edge. Make two.

2. Fold ½" to the wrong side on each long edge of the strap and press. Fold the strap in half lengthwise, wrong sides together, matching the pressed edges. Edgestitch ⅛" from each long edge of the strap.

3. Slide a metal D-ring onto each strap extender. Fold the extender in half, matching the raw edges, with the D-ring at the center fold. Make two.

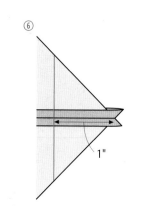

⑥

1"

4. Fold ½" to the wrong side on each end of the strap and press. Fold an additional ½" to the wrong side of each end and press again.

5. Slide a swivel clip onto each end of the strap, nestling it into the second crease. Sew a small rectangle on each end, enclosing the raw edges and securing the swivel clip. ⑤

Assemble the Exterior

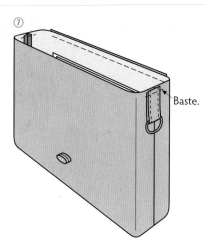

⑦

Baste.

1. Center the flap on the exterior back (the exterior panel with the zippered pocket) right sides together with raw edges aligned. Baste the raw edges together, using a ¼" seam allowance.

2. Place the exterior front and exterior back right sides together. Sew along the sides and bottom edge, leaving the top open. Trim the seam allowances to ¼" and press them open.

3. At the lower-left corner, fold the bag into a triangle shape, aligning the side and bottom seams. Measure 1" from the point and draw a line perpendicular to the seams. ⑥

4. Sew along the marked line to box the bag corner. Trim the seam allowances to ¼".

5. Repeat steps 3 and 4 at the lower-right corner. Turn the bag right side out.

6. Repeat steps 1–5 for the lining front and back, using a ⅝" seam allowance and leaving an 8" opening at the bottom of the lining for turning the bag right side out. Trim the seam allowances to ¼" and press.

7. Center one strap extender over the left side seam of the assembled exterior, aligning the raw edges. Baste the strap extender in place using a ¼" seam allowance. Repeat with the remaining strap extender and the right side seam. ⑦

Finish the Bag

1. Slip the lining over the exterior, right sides together. Be sure that the strap extenders and flap are tucked between the lining and exterior, and that the zippered pockets are on opposite sides of the bag. Match the side seams and pin in place.

2. Sew around the entire upper edge.

3. Turn the bag right side out through the opening in the lining. Press the seam allowances to the wrong side along the opening and either topstitch the opening closed by machine or slip-stitch it by hand. Press the bag well.

4. Topstitch ¼" from the top edge of the bag, keeping the flap out of the way.

5. Use the swivel clips to attach the strap to the metal D-rings.

A color variation of the Go-Go Bag

**Go-Go Bag
accent piece**
Cut 1 from aqua solid on fold.
Cut 1 from Shape-Flex on fold.

Place on fold.

½" seam allowance

MERINGUE CLUTCH

FINISHED BAG: 11" x 8½"

Ready for an evening out on the town? With this clutch, you definitely will be! The soft gathers give it an elegant look, and the straightforward design means you can sew it together in no time. In a pleasant afternoon of sewing, you can whip up a beautiful, modestly sized clutch to carry a few essentials along with you well into the evening.

Materials

Yardage is based on 42"-wide fabric.

⅝ yard of pink print for gathered panels

⅝ yard of pink solid for accents, foundation, lining, and strap

1⅛ yards of Shape-Flex fusible woven interfacing

⅜ yard of Décor Bond fusible interfacing

1 zipper, 14" long

1 metal swivel clip (¾" opening)

1 metal D-ring (¾")

Cutting

The patterns for the accent piece and main panel are on pages 37 and 38.

From the pink print, cut:
2 rectangles, 9" x 24", for gathered panels

From the solid pink, cut:
4 main panels, *on fold,* for foundation and lining fronts and backs
2 accent pieces, *on fold*
1 square, 2" x 2", for strap extender
1 rectangle, 2" x 15", for strap

From the Shape-Flex, cut:
4 main panels, *on fold*
2 accent pieces, *on fold*
1 square, 2" x 2", for strap extender
1 rectangle, 2" x 15", for strap

From the Décor Bond, cut:
2 main panels, *on fold;* trim ½" from all sides
2 accent pieces, *on fold;* trim ½" from all sides

Fuse the Fabrics and Interfacings

1. Fuse the Shape-Flex pieces to the wrong side of the corresponding fabric pieces for the foundation front and back, lining front and back, accents, strap, and strap extender.

2. Center the Décor Bond pieces on the interfaced side of the foundation front, foundation back, and both accent pieces, and fuse in place.

Make the Gathered Panels

All seam allowances are ½" unless otherwise noted.

1. Fold a gathered-panel rectangle in half along the vertical centerline and use a removable fabric marker to trace along the centerline. Repeat with the second rectangle and the front and back foundation pieces.

2. Stitch a line of gathering stitches ¼" from each long edge of each gathered-panel rectangle. Use a lengthened machine stitch (4.0 mm or 6 stitches per inch).

3. Place one gathered-panel rectangle on the foundation front, right sides up, with the centerlines matched. Pin, matching the raw edges.

4. Pull the bobbin threads of the gathering stitches to match the gathered panel to the foundation. Distribute the gathers evenly and pin in place. ①

5. Baste the outer edges of the bag using a ¼" seam allowance. Trim the corners of the gathered fabric to match the foundation.

6. Measure and mark a horizontal line 3" above the lower edge. Mark a second line 5½" above the lower edge. Topstitch along each line through the gathers and the foundation. ②

7. Repeat steps 3–6 with the remaining gathered-panel rectangle and the foundation back.

Attach the Accent Pieces

1. Stay stitch each accent piece ¼" from the lower (concave) edge. Clip the seam allowance along the curves, but do not clip the stitches. ③

2. Press the raw edge to the wrong side along the stitching on each piece.

3. Place the accent piece on the bag front, aligning the raw edges. Edgestitch ⅛" from the pressed edge to secure the accent piece to the bag. ④

4. Baste the raw edge of the accent piece to the bag front ¼" from the raw edge.

5. Repeat steps 3 and 4 with the remaining accent piece and the bag back.

Make the Strap

1. Fold the strap extender in half, wrong sides together, and press. Open the fabric and fold the raw edges in to meet at the crease; press. Refold along the original crease and press once again to make a tiny piece of double-fold tape. Edgestitch both long edges ⅛" from the folds.

2. Fold the strap in half lengthwise, wrong sides together, and repeat step 1 to complete the strap.

3. Slide the metal D-ring onto the strap extender. Fold the extender in half, matching the raw edges, with the D-ring at the fold.

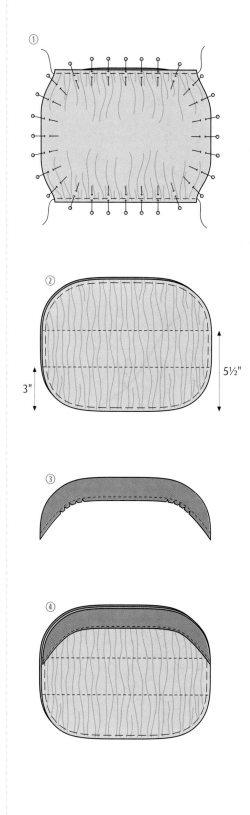

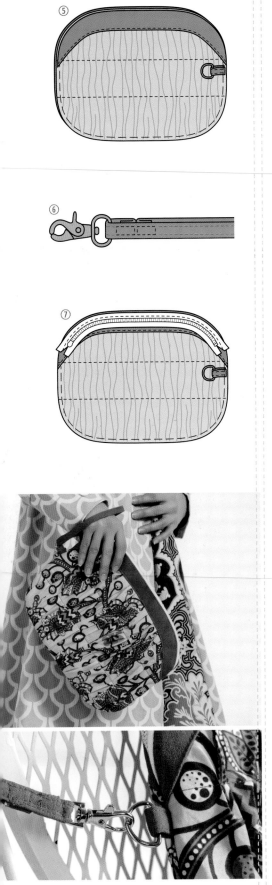

4. Baste the strap extender to the right side of the bag front, just below the accent, matching the raw edges. ⑤

5. Press ½" to the wrong side on each end of the strap. Slide the swivel clip onto the strap, 1" from one pressed end, and fold the strap around the swivel clip. Stitch ⅛" from the first fold, continuing along the previous stitches and across the strap just above the swivel clip to make a small rectangle, securing the strap end.

6. Bring the fold of the free end to meet the secured end, forming a loop. Stitch a rectangle on the second end as in step 5. ⑥

Attach the Zipper

1. With the bag front right side up, center the zipper right side down on the bag's upper edge, aligning the raw edges. Pin. Using a zipper foot, stitch the zipper to the bag front with a ¼" seam allowance. Taper both ends of the zipper tape off the edge of the bag front as you sew. ⑦

2. Place the lining front on the bag front, right sides together, and pin along the zipper edge. Sew directly on top of the previous stitching to join the lining and bag front.

3. Turn the fabrics right side out and press. Topstitch the bag front ⅛" from the zipper tape.

4. Repeat steps 1–3 to attach the bag back and lining to the other side of the zipper. Remove the zipper foot from your machine.

Finish the Bag

1. Unzip the zipper at least halfway. Open out the fabric pieces so that the exterior pieces are right sides together on one side of the zipper and the lining pieces are right sides together on the other side of the zipper. Pin in place, making sure the strap extender is tucked inside. Starting at one end of the zipper on the bag front/back, stitch around the edge of the exterior pieces using a ½" seam allowance.

2. Continue stitching around the lining fabrics, but use a ⅝" seam allowance. Leave a 6" opening along the bottom of the lining for turning.

> **Lining Fit**
> *Using a slightly wider seam allowance for the lining than the exterior will ensure a better fit in the finished bag.*

3. Turn the clutch right side out through the opening in the lining. Press the seam allowance to the wrong side along the opening and either topstitch the opening closed by machine or slip-stitch it by hand. Press the clutch seams well for a nicely finished look, but take care not to flatten the gathers.

4. Clip the strap to the strap extender.

Meringue Clutch accent piece
Cut 2 from solid pink on fold.
Cut 2 from Shape-Flex on fold.
Cut 2 from Décor Bond on fold.

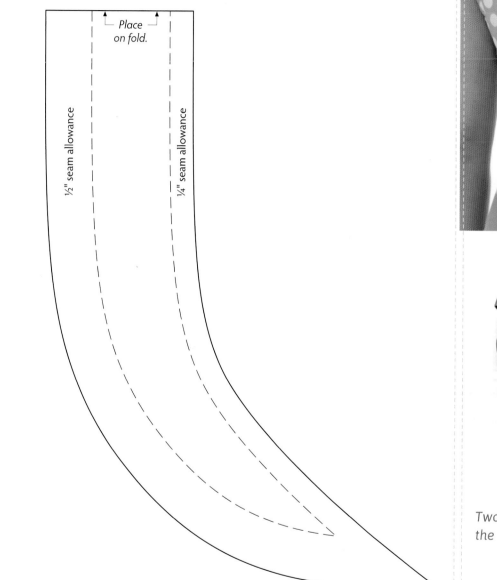

Place on fold.

½" seam allowance

¼" seam allowance

Two color variations of the Meringue Clutch

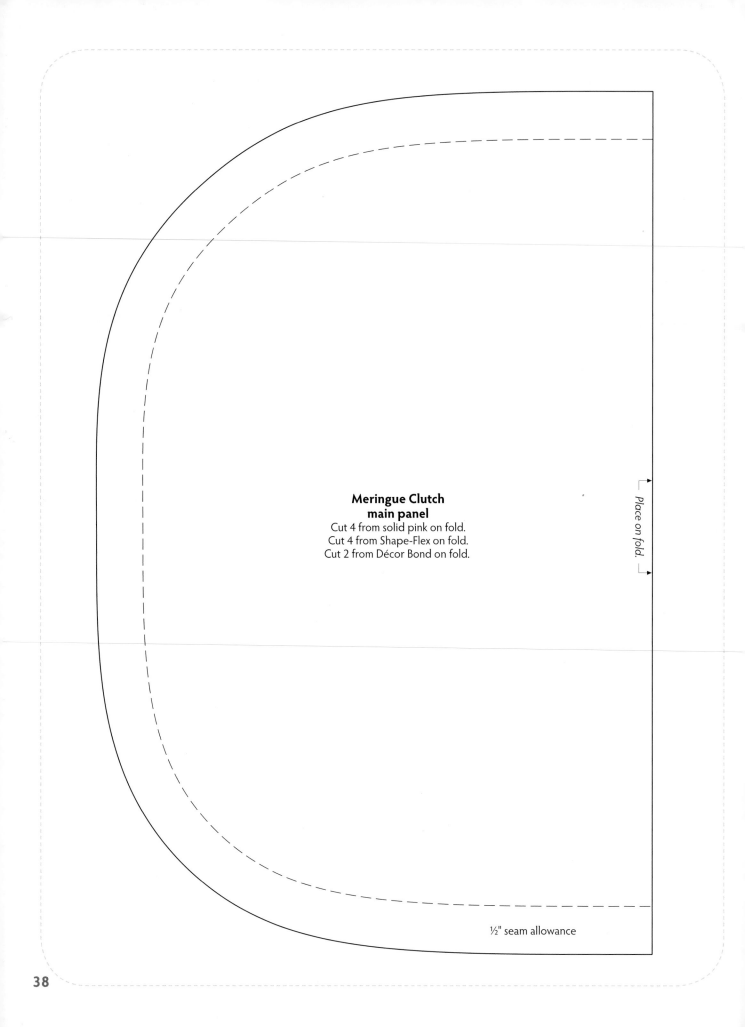

Meringue Clutch
main panel
Cut 4 from solid pink on fold.
Cut 4 from Shape-Flex on fold.
Cut 2 from Décor Bond on fold.

Place on fold.

½" seam allowance

WONDERLAND BAG

FINISHED BAG: 11" x 7½" x 6"

Take a trip down the rabbit hole with this slick bag. It features piping and leather handles, with a sweet rounded front. The construction comes together quickly, so you'll never be late for a very important date!

Materials

Yardage is based on 42"-wide fabric.

¾ yard of multicolored print for exterior

1 yard of fabric for lining

1 fat quarter *or* ¼ yard of blue solid for piping

½ yard of Deco-Fuse fusible interfacing

¾ yard of Thermolam Plus fusible fleece

1½ yards of Shape-Flex fusible woven interfacing

1½ yards of ¼"-wide cotton cording

1 pair of 28" leather handles with prepunched tabs

1 zipper, 10" long

Tapestry or heavyweight thread*

*Or use double- or triple-strand of regular thread

Cutting

The pattern for the side panel is on page 43.

From the multicolored print, cut:
2 side panels, *on fold*
2 rectangles, 11½" x 12½", for exterior front and back
1 rectangle, 8" x 11½", for exterior bottom

From the lining fabric, cut:
2 side panels, *on fold*
2 rectangles, 11½" x 12½", for lining front and back
1 rectangle, 8" x 11½", for lining bottom
4 rectangles, 6" x 12½", for pockets

From the blue solid, cut *on the bias:*
Enough 1½"-wide strips to equal 60" in length, piecing as necessary

From the Deco-Fuse, cut:
2 side panels, *on fold;* trim ½" from all edges
1 rectangle, 7" x 10½", for bottom

From the Thermolam Plus, cut:
2 side panels, *on fold*
2 rectangles, 11½" x 12½", for exterior front and back
1 rectangle, 8" x 11½", for exterior bottom

From the Shape-Flex, cut:
2 side panels, *on fold*
2 rectangles, 11½" x 12½", for lining front and back
1 rectangle, 8" x 11½", for lining bottom
4 rectangles, 6" x 12½", for pockets

Fuse the Fabrics and Interfacings

1. Fuse the Thermolam Plus pieces to the wrong side of the corresponding fabric pieces for the exterior sides, front, back, and bottom.

2. Center the Deco-Fuse pieces on the interfaced side of the exterior sides and bottom and fuse in place.

3. Fuse the Shape-Flex pieces to the wrong side of the corresponding pieces for the lining sides, front, back, bottom, and pockets.

Attach the Zipper

All seam allowances are ½" unless otherwise noted.

1. Align the exterior front and back, right sides together. With a removable fabric marker, make a mark 1" from each end of one 11½" edge; this will be the top of the bag. Using a ⅝" seam allowance, sew from each mark to the nearest side edge; each line of stitching will be only 1" long. ①

2. Set the machine for a long straight stitch (4.0 mm or 6 stitches per inch). Baste between the two lines of stitching from the previous step, using a ⅝" seam allowance. Press open the seam allowances along the entire seam.

3. Insert the zipper, following the instructions in "Zipper Panel" on page 13.

4. Repeat step 1 with the lining front and back. Then, rather than basting between the 1" lines of stitching, press the seam allowances to the wrong side along the gap.

Assemble the Exterior and Handle

1. Mark placements for the handle tabs 4½" below the zipper and 3½" from the side edges of the exterior front and back. Alter the position as necessary for the specific handles you've chosen. Referring to "Leather Handles" on page 19, hand sew each tab in place. ②

2. Fold the blue bias strip, right side out, around the cotton cording, matching the raw edges. Using a zipper foot, sew ¼" from the raw edges of the bias tape. ③

3. Position the prepared piping along one side edge of the bag exterior, with the raw edges matched. Taper the piping slightly off the bag edge at the ends (the bottom of the bag). Pin in place.

4. With the zipper foot, baste the piping in place. The basting should lie on top of the previous stitches. Trim the excess piping. Repeat to add piping to the other side of the bag exterior. ④

5. Mark the center of one bag side at the curved upper edge. Matching the mark to the zipper seam, pin the bag side to the bag exterior, right sides together and raw edges aligned. With a zipper or piping foot, sew along the piped edge from the marked center toward the bottom corner. Stop sewing and backstitch ½" before reaching the lower raw edges. Reposition the bag and sew from the mark to ½" above the raw

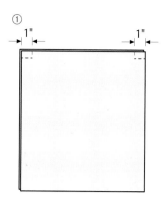

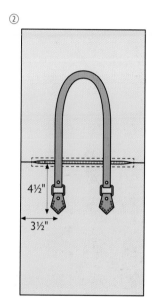

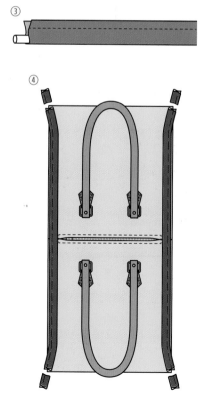

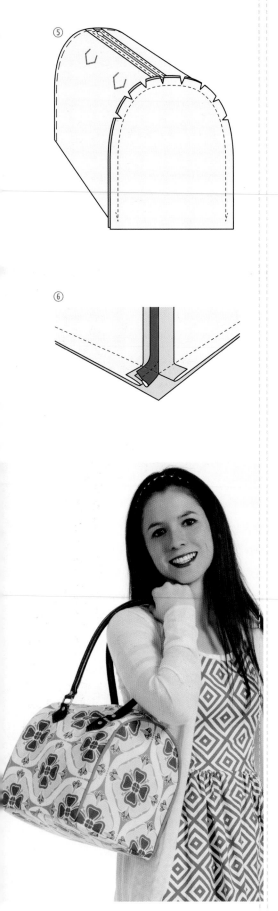

⑤

edges at the opposite corner. The ½" seam allowance sandwiches the piping tightly between the bag pieces. Cut small V-shaped notches in the seam allowances along the curve, being careful not to cut into the stitches of the seam line. ⑤

6. Repeat to sew the remaining bag side to the bag exterior. Remove the zipper foot.

7. Unzip the zipper. With the bag exterior still wrong side out, pin the bag bottom to the assembled unit, matching the raw edges. The unsewn ½" at the bottom of each side seam will open up at the corners of the bag bottom. Pin and then sew the bottom to the bag. Trim the corners diagonally to reduce bulk, being careful not to cut into the stitches. ⑥

8. Turn the bag right side out through the zipper opening. Press well.

Assemble the Lining and Pockets

1. Place two pocket pieces right sides together and sew along one 12½" edge. Press the seam allowances open. Fold the pocket right side out along the seam and press again. Topstitch ¼" from the sewn edge for the top of the pocket.

2. Place the pocket on the lining front, aligning the lower raw edges, and baste along the three raw edges.

3. Finger-press a vertical crease by folding the pocket and lining front in half. Open the unit and topstitch on the crease from the top of the pocket to the lower edge, dividing the pocket into two sections.

4. Repeat steps 1–3 to make a second pocket and attach it to the lining back.

5. Mark the center of the curved upper edge of one lining side. Aligning the raw edges and matching the center to the top seam in the lining, sew the side piece to one long edge of the assembled lining body using a ⅝" seam allowance. Stop sewing and backstitch ⅝" from the lower edges of the bag and side pieces. Clip the seam allowances along the curve, being careful not to cut into the stitches. Repeat to attach the remaining lining side to the other edge of the lining front/back.

6. Attach the lining bottom as you did for the exterior bag pieces, but use a ⅝" seam allowance.

Lining Seams
Using a slightly wider seam allowance for the lining than the exterior will ensure a better fit in the finished bag.

Finish the Bag

1. Place the lining inside the bag exterior, wrong sides together. Slip-stitch the opening in the lining to the zipper tape by hand.

2. With wrong sides together, press the bag well for a nicely finished look, pressing creases along the seam lines.

Pattern does include seam allowances.

**Wonderland Bag
side panel**
Cut 2 from multicolored print on fold.
Cut 2 from lining fabric on fold.
Cut 2 from Deco-Fuse on fold.
Cut 2 from Thermolam Plus on fold.
Cut 2 from Shape-Flex on fold.

Place on fold.

½" seam allowance

*A color variation of the
Wonderland Bag*

BEE SWEET BAG

FINISHED BAG: 14" x 11"

Sturdy yet beautiful, this bag will definitely turn heads. Many great features, from the chiseled flap to the leather handles, work together to create a unique look. The bag also offers inner pockets and an adjustable strap. Whether for business or pleasure, you will be able to tote your files (or favorite novel) in great style. Use a fabulous large-print fabric for this one.

Materials

Yardage is based on 42"-wide fabric.

1 yard of green print for exterior
1 yard of aqua print for lining
⅛ yard of aqua solid for accent
1¾ yards of Shape-Flex fusible woven interfacing
⅞ yard of Deco-Fuse fusible interfacing (or substitute Peltex One-Sided Fusible)
¾ yard of Thermolam Plus fusible fleece
1 magnetic snap (½")
1 pair of 28" leather handles with prepunched tabs
1 metal rectangle ring (1½")
1 metal slider (1½")
Tapestry or heavyweight thread*

Or use double- or triple-strand of regular thread

Cutting

The patterns for the flap accent and flap are on pages 49 and 50.

From the green print, cut:
1 rectangle, 4" x 42", for strap
1 square, 4" x 4", for strap extender
2 rectangles, 12" x 15", for exterior front and back
2 rectangles, 5" x 12", for exterior sides
1 rectangle, 5" x 15", for exterior bottom
1 flap, *on fold*

From the aqua print, cut:
2 rectangles, 12" x 15", for lining front and back
2 rectangles, 5" x 12", for lining sides
1 rectangle, 5" x 15", for lining bottom
2 rectangles, 8" x 16", for pockets
1 flap, *on fold*, for flap lining

From the aqua solid, cut:
1 flap accent, *on fold*

From the Shape-Flex, cut:
1 rectangle, 4" x 42", for strap
1 square, 4" x 4", for strap extender
2 rectangles, 12" x 15", for lining front and back
2 rectangles, 5" x 12", for lining sides
1 rectangle, 5" x 15", for lining bottom
2 rectangles, 8" x 16", for pockets
1 flap accent, *on fold*

Continued on page 46

"Cutting" continued from page 45

From the Thermolam Plus, cut:
2 rectangles, 12" x 15", for exterior front and back
2 rectangles, 5" x 12", for exterior sides
1 rectangle, 5" x 15", for exterior bottom
2 flaps, *on fold*

From the Deco-Fuse, cut:
2 rectangles, 11" x 14", for exterior front and back
1 rectangle, 4" x 14", for exterior bottom

Fuse the Fabrics and Interfacings

1. Fuse the Shape-Flex pieces to the wrong side of the corresponding fabric pieces for the strap; strap extender; lining front, back, sides, and bottom; pockets; and flap accent.

2. Fuse the Thermolam Plus pieces to the wrong side of the corresponding pieces for the exterior front, back, sides, bottom, and flap, as well as the lining flap.

3. Center the Deco-Fuse pieces on the interfaced side of the exterior front, back, and bottom and fuse in place.

Assemble the Flap

All seam allowances are ½" unless otherwise noted.

1. Place the flap accent on the exterior flap, right sides up, aligning the raw edges at the bottom and sides of the flap. Pin generously.

2. Set the machine for a blanket stitch 3.5 mm wide and 2.5 mm long or a satin zigzag stitch 3.0 mm wide and 1.0 mm long. Sew along the upper edge of the accent, allowing the stitch to overcast, or wrap around, the raw edge. With a straight stitch, baste the side and lower edges of the flap accent to the flap, sewing ¼" from the raw edges.

3. Finger-press the lining flap in half, lengthwise, to find the center. Make a mark on the centerline, 5½" below the straight upper edge.

4. Insert the thinner part of the magnetic snap at the mark, referring to "Magnetic Snaps" on page 16.

5. Place the assembled exterior and lining flaps right sides together. Sew the entire outer edge, leaving a 6" opening along the long straight edge for turning.

6. Trim the seam allowances to ¼". Trim the corners diagonally to reduce bulk and clip along the curved edges, being careful not to cut into the stitches. Turn right side out and press, turning the seam allowances to the wrong side along the opening.

7. Edgestitch ⅛" from the sides and shaped lower edge of the flap, leaving the long straight edge unsewn.

Make the Pockets

1. Fold a pocket piece in half, right sides together, matching the short edges. Sew along the raw edges, leaving a 3" opening opposite the fold for turning. ①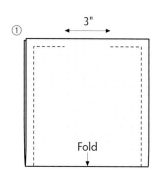

2. Trim the corners diagonally to reduce bulk. Turn the pocket right side out and press, folding the seam allowances to the wrong side along the opening.

3. Topstitch ¼" from the folded edge of the pocket.

4. With the topstitched folded edge as the top of the pocket, finger-press the pocket in half to mark the vertical centerline. Do the same for the lining front.

5. Place the pocket on the lining front, right sides up, with the centerlines matching and the pocket's lower edge 2" above the lower edge of the lining. Pin in place. ②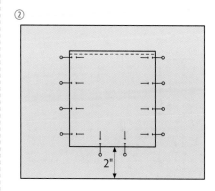

6. Edgestitch ⅛" from the pocket's sides and lower edge, closing the opening as you sew.

7. Repeat steps 1–6 to make the second pocket and attach it to the lining back.

Attach the Snap and Handles

1. Mark the snap placement on the exterior front, centered 2" below the bag's upper edge. Insert the remaining half of the magnetic snap, referring to "Magnetic Snaps."

2. Temporarily snap the assembled flap to the bag front. Using one of the leather handles as a guide, mark the placements for the leather handle tabs below the flap cutouts. Be sure that the tabs are positioned to allow the flap to open and close freely. Trace an outline of each tab with a removable fabric marker.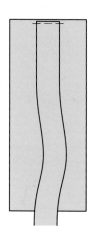

3. Remove the handle and flap. Measure the distance of each placement mark from the bag's upper and side edges. Use the measurements to mark handle-tab placements on the bag back.

4. Referring to "Leather Handles" on page 19, hand sew each tab in place.

Make the Strap

1. Press ½" to the wrong side along each long edge of the strap. Fold the strap in half lengthwise, matching the folded edges, and press. Edgestitch ⅛" from each long edge. Prepare the strap extender in the same way.

2. Assemble the strap and strap extender, referring to "Metal Slider for an Adjustable Strap" on page 17. Center the strap and strap extender along the upper edges of the bag side pieces and baste in place. ③

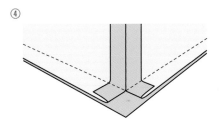

④

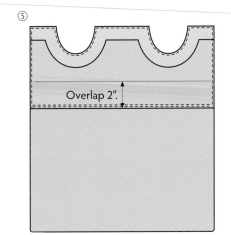

⑤

Overlap 2".

A color variation of the Bee Sweet Bag

Assemble the Exterior

1. Place the exterior front and one exterior side right sides together, matching the raw edges along one short edge of the bag front. Sew the side seam from the upper edge to a point ½" from the lower raw edges, backstitch, and press the seam allowances open. Repeat to join the exterior back to the free edge of the exterior side.

2. Sew the remaining exterior side to the free edges of the front and back panels in the same way. Press the seam allowances open. You will have a rectangular tube of fabric.

3. With the exterior panels still wrong side out, align the corners and edges with the exterior bottom and pin in place. The ½" left unsewn at the end of each side seam will open up at the corners of the exterior bottom. Sew around the entire bottom, pivoting at the corners. Trim the corners diagonally to reduce bulk, being careful not to cut into the stitches. ④

4. Turn the bag exterior right side out.

5. Repeat steps 1–3 to assemble the lining pieces. Leave a 6" opening in the seam joining the lining back to the bottom for turning. Be sure both pocket openings face the top of the assembled lining.

6. Moving the handles out of the way, draw a line 2" from the top edge of the exterior back (the panel without the magnetic snap). Place the long straight edge of the flap along the line, centering the flap on the exterior back. ⑤

7. Topstitch the flap to the exterior back ⅛" and ¼" from the long straight edge of the flap.

Finish the Bag

1. Slip the lining over the exterior, right sides together. Tuck the handles and flap between the layers. Pin the lining to the bag along the upper edge, matching the side seams. Sew the entire upper edge.

2. Turn the bag right side out through the opening in the lining. Press the top edge along the seam line. To keep the lining from rolling to the right side along the seam, you may choose to topstitch ¼" from the pressed edge through all the layers.

3. Press the seam allowances to the wrong side along the opening in the lining. Close the opening with machine topstitching or slip-stitch by hand. Press the bag well for a nicely finished look.

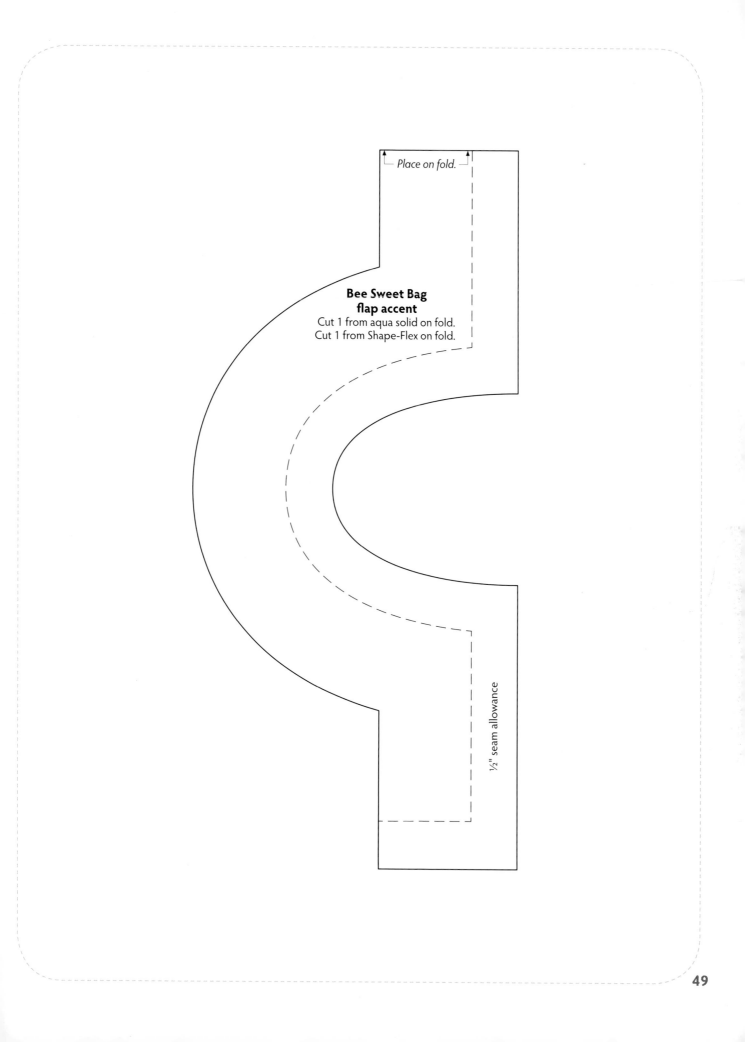

Place on fold.

**Bee Sweet Bag
flap accent**
Cut 1 from aqua solid on fold.
Cut 1 from Shape-Flex on fold.

½" seam allowance

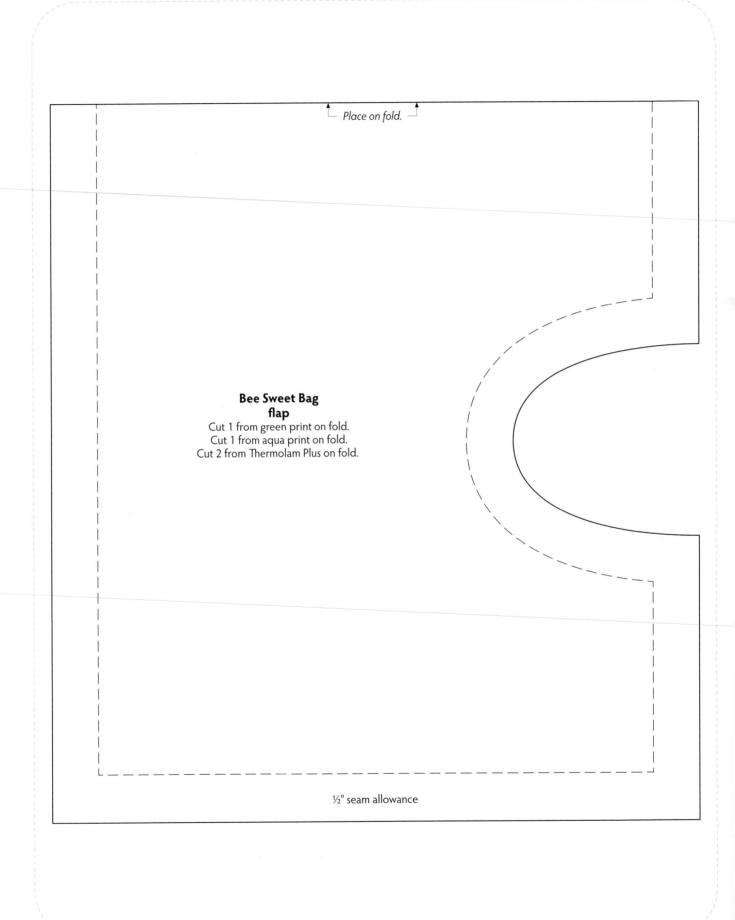

Place on fold.

**Bee Sweet Bag
flap**
Cut 1 from green print on fold.
Cut 1 from aqua print on fold.
Cut 2 from Thermolam Plus on fold.

½" seam allowance

50

OH SPIT! DIAPER BAG

FINISHED BAG: 17" x 12" x 5" • CHANGING PAD: 19" x 27"
Now you can bypass the usual frumpy diaper bag and head out with this stylish, modern version, which also doubles as a cool purse. This diaper bag has several pockets and compartments to keep Mom's and Baby's things separate, yet still easily accessible. Also included are instructions for a handy changing pad. Because the pattern uses several different fabrics, you can feature your favorite fabric line in style.

Materials

Yardage is based on 42"-wide fabric.

1⅝ yards of blue large-scale print for bag exterior and changing pad

¾ yard of green solid for bag straps and zipper panel

½ yard of PUL (polyurethane laminated fabric) or other water-resistant fabric for changing pad

¼ yard *or* 1 fat quarter of animal print for bag front pocket

1½ yards of blue-and-white print for bag lining

5 yards of Shape-Flex fusible woven interfacing

1⅛ yards of Thermolam Plus fusible fleece

3 packages (3 yards each) of ½"-wide double-fold bias tape

¼ yard of ¾"-wide knit elastic

1 sport zipper, 16" long

4 metal rectangle rings (1½")

Optional: 4 metal purse feet

Cutting

From the blue large-scale print, cut:
1 rectangle, 19" x 27", for changing pad
2 rectangles, 13" x 18", for exterior front and back
2 rectangles, 9" x 18", for exterior back pocket
1 rectangle, 6" x 18", for exterior bottom
2 rectangles, 7" x 12½", for exterior sides
4 rectangles, 7" x 10½", for exterior side pockets

From the green solid, cut:
2 rectangles, 4" x 30", for straps
4 rectangles, 4" x 14", for strap extenders
4 rectangles, 3½" x 17", for zipper side panels
4 rectangles, 1½" x 7", for zipper end panels

From the blue-and-white print, cut:
2 rectangles, 13" x 18", for lining front and back
1 rectangle, 6" x 18", for lining bottom
4 rectangles, 10 x 18", for dividers
2 rectangles, 7" x 12½", for lining sides

From the animal print, cut:
2 rectangles, 4½" x 18", for exterior front pocket

From the PUL, cut:
1 rectangle, 19" x 27", for changing pad

From the Thermolam Plus, cut:
1 rectangle, 19" x 27", for changing pad
2 rectangles, 13" x 18", for exterior front and back
1 rectangle, 6" x 18", for exterior bottom
2 rectangles, 7" x 12½", for exterior sides

Continued on page 53

"Cutting" continued from page 51

From the Shape-Flex, cut:
2 rectangles, 13" x 18", for lining front and back
2 rectangles, 7" x 12½", for lining sides
1 rectangle, 6" x 18", for lining bottom
2 rectangles, 9" x 18", for back pocket
4 rectangles, 7" x 10½", for side pockets
2 rectangles, 4½" x 18", for front pocket
4 rectangles, 3½" x 17", for zipper side panels
4 rectangles, 1½" x 7", for zipper end panels
4 rectangles, 10" x 18", for dividers
2 rectangles, 4" x 30", for straps
4 rectangles, 4" x 14", for strap extenders

Fuse the Fabrics and Interfacings

1. Fuse the appropriate pieces of Thermolam Plus to the wrong side of the print changing-pad rectangle and the exterior front, back, bottom, and sides.

2. Fuse the Shape-Flex pieces to the wrong side of the corresponding fabric pieces for the back, side, and front pockets; zipper side and end panels; dividers; strap and strap extenders; and lining front, back, sides, and bottom.

Make the Changing Pad

All seam allowances are ½" unless otherwise noted.

1. Using a removable marker, trace a drinking glass or other round object at all four corners of the changing-pad pieces. Cut along the curved lines. Position the changing-pad pieces with wrong sides together and raw edges matched.

2. To make the tie closure, cut two 12" lengths of double-fold bias tape. Open one tape, fold ¼" to the wrong side on one short end, and press. Refold the tape along the original creases and press again. Edgestitch the tape along both long edges and the folded end. Repeat to finish the second length of tape.

3. Place the prepared bias tapes on top of each other, matching the raw edges. Position the tapes on the main fabric right side, centered on one short end, with the raw edges matching. Baste ¼" from the raw edges.

Top: Changing pads, rolled and unrolled

Bottom: A color variation of the Oh Spit! Diaper Bag

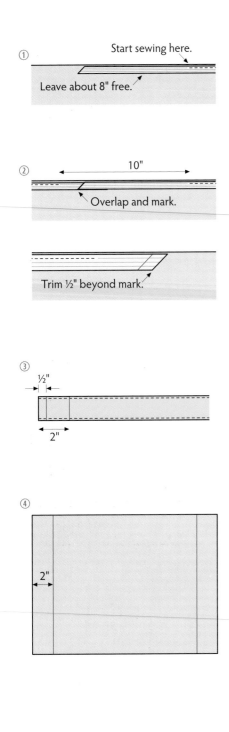

① Start sewing here.

Leave about 8" free.

② 10"

Overlap and mark.

Trim ½" beyond mark.

③ ½"

2"

④ 2"

Tale of the Tape

You'll need about 2½ yards of double-fold bias tape to bind the changing pad. You may choose to begin with a fresh 3-yard package of bias tape or continue with the partially used package. If necessary, join a new length of bias tape to the original one by opening the folded tapes and stitching the ends together. Use a ¼" seam allowance and sew with right sides together. Press the seam allowances open to reduce bulk at the join, refold the tape, and press again along the original creases.

4. Open the remainder of the bias tape and cut one end at a 45° angle. Pin the tape to the changing pad with right sides together, matching the raw edges. Begin near the center of one long side and leave about 8" of the tape free for joining later. Sew the tape to the changing pad along the crease closest to the raw edges. ①

5. Stop sewing about 10" from the beginning of stitching. Arrange the ends of the bias tape along the remaining edge of the changing pad so that the beginning overlaps the end of the tape. Mark the end of the tape where the angled beginning falls and then cut the tape ½" beyond the line for seam allowance. Match the ends of the tape and sew a ¼" seam; press the seam allowances open. Finish sewing the tape to the changing pad. ②

6. Refold the bias tape along its original creases, wrapping the tape around the edges of the changing pad. Pin the folded tape to the wrong side of the changing pad so that it covers the line of stitches, and then sew the binding in place from the right side by machine stitching in the ditch.

7. Roll up the changing pad, wrap the bias-tape ties around the roll, and tie to secure.

Make the Bag Straps

1. Press ½" to the wrong side along each long edge of a strap. Fold the strap in half lengthwise, matching the folded edges and concealing the long raw edges. Press and then edgestitch ⅛" from each long edge. Make two.

2. Repeat step 1 to make four strap extenders.

3. Measure and mark each strap extender ½" and 2" from one short end. Press the strap extender to the wrong side at each mark. Measure, mark, and press both ends of each strap in the same way. ③

4. Slide a metal rectangle ring onto each strap extender and nestle it into the crease at the 2" mark. Pin the strap extender around the ring. Make four.

5. Measure and mark lines 2" from each side of the bag front and bag back for strap placement. ④

6. Place a strap along one placement line on the bag front, with the outer edge of the strap extender along the line. The pressed edges of the extender should lie against the right side of the bag fabric. Align the raw edge of the strap extender with the lower raw edge of the bag front. Pin in place. Repeat to position the remaining bag extenders at the other placement lines on the bag front and back.

7. Topstitch the strap extenders to the bag pieces. Begin sewing at the lower edge of one strap extender, and sew directly on top of the previous stitches. Sew as close to the metal ring as possible, and then pivot and sew across the strap extender. Pivot again and sew along the previous stitches, down the opposite side of the strap extender, to the bag's lower edge. Repeat to attach the remaining three strap extenders. ⑤

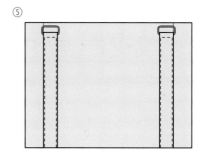

Make the Bag Pockets

1. Place the back pocket pieces wrong sides together. Referring to the instructions for the changing pad on pages 53 and 54, bind one long edge of the pocket with bias tape; this will be the top edge.

2. Repeat step 1 to make the front pocket and two side pockets.

3. Position the back pocket on the exterior back, right sides up, over the strap extenders. Baste the lower edges together using a ¼" seam allowance. ⑥

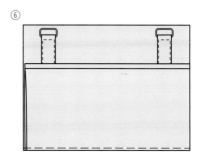

4. Position the front pocket on the exterior front as in step 3. Fold the unit in half lengthwise and finger-press a crease along the center of the pocket. Sew along the crease, backstitching at the pocket's upper edge to reinforce the seam. ⑦

5. Topstitch each assembled side pocket 1" below the bias tape. Sewing through both layers creates a casing for the elastic. ⑧

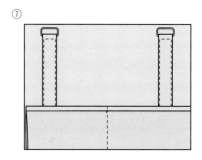

6. Cut two 4" pieces of elastic. Attach a safety pin to one end of an elastic length and feed it through the casing on one side pocket. Remove the pin and arrange the elastic so the ends are even with the raw edges of the pocket. Baste each end of the elastic in place ⅛" from the raw edges. Repeat with the second piece of elastic and the remaining side pocket.

7. Place a side pocket on each exterior side panel, matching the sides and lower edges and pin securely. Use a drinking glass to trace a curve at each of the bottom corners; then baste using a ¼" seam allowance. Trim the corners along the curves. ⑨

Assemble the Bag Exterior

1. To add the optional purse feet, refer to "Purse Feet" on page 16.

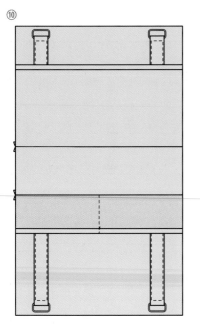

2. Sew the assembled exterior front to the exterior bottom along one long edge. Press the seam allowances open. Stitch the assembled exterior back to the remaining long edge of the exterior bottom. ⑩

3. Sew one bag side panel to the assembled bag exterior, matching the upper edges. Pin the pieces together first and distribute the fabric evenly along the exterior bottom. Repeat to attach the remaining exterior side. ⑪

On the Side

I recommend sewing from the upper edge toward the bottom of the bag when attaching the side pieces. Sewing the bottom edge last makes it easier to evenly distribute the fullness.

4. Clip the seam allowances along the curves, being careful not to cut into the stitches. Turn the bag right side out and press.

Attach the Zipper

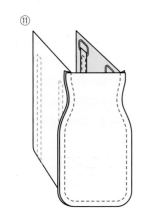

1. Place the zipper on one zipper side panel, right sides together, with the zipper centered and aligned with one long edge of the panel. Using a zipper foot, sew with a ¼" seam allowance.

2. Position a second zipper side panel on the first, right sides together, with the zipper between the fabric layers. Pin the layers together. Sew directly on top of the previous stitches.

3. Press both side panels away from the zipper. Edgestitch the side panels close to the seam. ⑫

4. Repeat steps 1–3 to attach the remaining zipper side panels to the other side of the zipper.

5. Sew a zipper end panel to one short end of the assembled zipper unit, right sides together. Position a second end panel on the first, right sides together, with the zipper unit sandwiched between the end panels. Sew again along the previous stitches. Press both end panels away from the zipper unit. Edgestitch close to the seam. ⑬

6. Repeat step 5 to attach the remaining zipper end panels to the other end of the zipper unit.

Assemble the Dividers

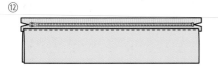

1. Place two dividers right sides together and sew all around the edges, leaving a 3" opening for turning. Trim the corners diagonally to reduce bulk, turn the divider right side out, and press, turning the seam allowances to the wrong side along the opening.

2. Edgestitch ⅛" from all the edges.

3. Fold one 18" edge up by 3½" and press. ⑭

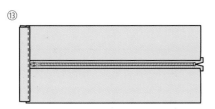

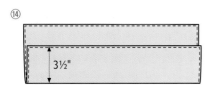

3½"

4. Place the completed divider on the lining front, right sides up, with the folded edge of the divider ½" above the lower edge of the lining and the sides of the divider ½" inside the lining raw edges. Topstitch the sides and folded lower edge of the divider to the lining, ¼" from the divider edges. ⑮

5. Measure 6" from the left edge of the lining and draw a vertical line across the divider with a removable marker. Sew on the line to separate the divider into sections, backstitching to reinforce the seam ends. ⑯

6. Repeat steps 1–5 to assemble the second divider and attach it to the lining back.

Assemble the Lining

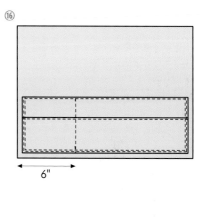

1. Cut 1" from the top edges of the lining front, back, and sides. Do not discard. Curve the bottom corners of the lining sides as for the exterior pieces. ⑰

2. Place the assembled zipper panel on the lining front with the right sides of both pieces face up. Position the 1" slice of the lining front on the other pieces, right side down, so the zipper panel is between the lining pieces. Sew the top edge, using a ¼" seam allowance. Open the fabric away from the zipper panel and press. ⑱

3. Repeat step 2 to attach the lining back pieces to the opposite long edge of the zipper panel.

4. Sew the lining sides to the short ends of the zipper panel in the same way. Begin and end the seams ½" from the fabric raw edges so that the previous seam line is not crossed, and use a ¼" seam allowance. Open the fabric away from the zipper and press. Unzip the zipper.

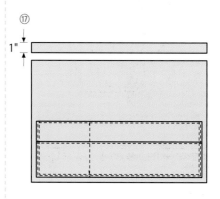

5. Sew the lower edge of the lining front to one long edge of the lining bottom. In the same manner, sew the lining back to the remaining long edge of the lining bottom. Press the seam allowances open.

6. Stitch the lining sides to the assembled lining front/bottom/back. Pin first, and distribute the fullness evenly around the curves and bottom edges.

7. Clip the seam allowances along the curves, being careful not to cut into the stitches, and press.

Finish the Bag

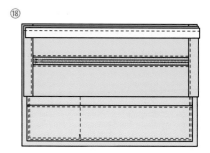

1. Place the lining inside the exterior, wrong sides together, and pin in place, matching the centers and the side seams.

2. Bind the raw edges of the bag as you did for the changing pad.

3. Attach each strap end to one of the metal rings on the bag. Position a ring in the crease 2" from one strap end and pin the end, with ½" folded to the wrong side, to the strap, enclosing the ring. Topstitch a small rectangle through the strap layers to secure the end of the strap. Repeat to secure the remaining strap ends, taking care not to twist the straps.

LUCKY DENVER MINT BAG

FINISHED BAG: 12½" x 14" with flap extended
This soft bag is as comfortable as your most-washed pair of jeans. The zippered top can be folded down as a flap, or positioned straight up for more storage, making this a unique, convertible way to tote around all your essentials.

Materials

Yardage is based on 42"-wide fabric.

⅝ yard of pink-and-brown print for exterior
⅝ yard of purple print for lining
½ yard of blue solid for straps
1 yard of Shape-Flex fusible woven interfacing
1 yard of Thermolam Plus fusible fleece
1 zipper, 18" long
4 metal O-rings (1½")

Straight Up

Fabric yardage is sufficient to cut the bag panels on the lengthwise grain, allowing you to take advantage of large-scale prints.

Cutting

From the pink-and-brown print, cut:
2 rectangles, 14" x 16¾", for exterior front and back*

From the purple print, cut:
2 rectangles, 14" x 16¾", for lining front and back*
2 rectangles, 8" x 10", for pockets

From the blue solid, cut:
2 rectangles, 4" x 24", for straps
4 rectangles, 4" x 11", for strap extenders

From the Shape-Flex, cut:
2 rectangles, 4" x 24", for straps
4 rectangles, 4" x 11", for strap extenders
2 rectangles, 8" x 10", for pockets

From the Thermolam Plus, cut:
4 rectangles, 14" x 16¾", for exterior and lining fronts and backs*

After cutting the front and back rectangles, use the pattern on page 63 to trim the upper edge of each rectangle into a curved shape.

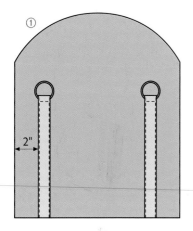

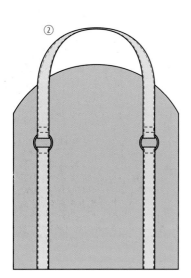

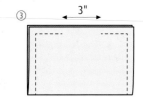

Fuse the Fabrics and Interfacings

1. Fuse the Shape-Flex pieces to the wrong side of the corresponding fabric pieces for the straps, strap extenders, and pockets.

2. Fuse the Thermolam Plus pieces to the wrong side of the corresponding pieces for the exterior and lining fronts and backs.

Make and Attach the Straps

All seam allowances are ½" unless otherwise noted.

1. Fold one strap in half lengthwise, wrong sides together, and press. Open the strap and fold both long ends to meet at the center crease; press. Refold the strap along the original crease and press once more, enclosing the long edges. Edgestitch ⅛" from each long edge of the strap. Prepare the second strap and all four strap extenders in the same way.

2. Press 1" to the wrong side on one short edge of each strap extender. Slide an O-ring onto the crease of each extender.

3. With a removable marker, draw vertical lines 2" from each side of the bag front and back panels.

4. Place one strap extender along one placement line on the exterior front, with the outer edge of the strap extender along the line. Align the raw edges at the bottom of the bag. Pin the strap extender to the bag. Stitch the extender to the bag, sewing on top of the previous stitches. Sew as close to the O-ring as possible, keeping the raw edge tucked between the strap extender and the bag. Stop with the needle down and pivot; sew across the strap extender just below the O-ring. Pivot again and sew along the remaining long edge of the extender. Repeat to attach the remaining strap extenders along the remaining lines on the exterior front and back. ①

5. Press ½" to the wrong side on one short end of a strap. Press an additional 1" to the wrong side. Repeat at the remaining short end of the strap and on both ends of the second strap.

6. Slide a strap through the ring on one side of the exterior front, folding the strap around the ring at the second crease. Sew a small rectangle near the strap end, enclosing the raw edge against the handle. Repeat to attach the other end of the handle to the second ring on the exterior front. Attach the second handle to the exterior back. ②

Make the Pockets

1. Fold one pocket piece in half widthwise, right sides together, to make a 5" x 8" rectangle. Sew along the three raw edges, leaving a 3" opening opposite the fold for turning. ③

2. Trim the corners diagonally to reduce bulk. Turn the pocket right side out and press. Topstitch ¼" from the folded edge of the pocket. Make two.

3. With the topstitched edge as the top of the pocket, finger-press one pocket in half to mark the vertical center. Do the same for the lining front.

4. Place the pocket on the lining front, right sides up, with the centerlines matched and the pocket's lower edge 2" above the lower raw edge of the lining front. Pin in place. ④

5. Edgestitch ⅛" from the pocket's sides and lower edge, closing the opening as you sew.

6. Repeat steps 3–5 to attach the remaining pocket to the lining back.

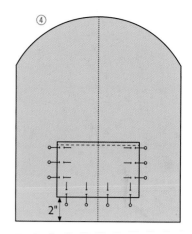
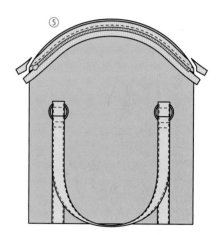

Attach the Zipper

1. Place the zipper on the exterior front, right sides together. Center the zipper on the bag's curved upper edge and align the zipper tape with the bag's raw edges. Pin in place. Using a zipper foot, stitch the zipper to the bag with a ¼" seam allowance, tapering both ends of the zipper slightly off the edge of the exterior front so the raw edges of the zipper tape are concealed in the seam. Trim the excess from the sides of the bag, being careful not to cut off the zipper pull. ⑤

2. Pin the lining front to the exterior front along the upper edge, right sides together, with the zipper between the fabric layers. Sew directly on top of the previous stitching. Notch the seam allowances along the curved edges, being careful not to cut into the stitches.

3. Turn the fronts right side out and press. Edgestitch along the curved edge, ⅛" from the zipper tape.

4. Repeat steps 1–3 to attach the exterior and lining backs to the other side of the zipper. Remove the zipper foot from the machine.

Finish the Bag

1. Unzip the zipper. Place the exterior front and exterior back right sides together and stitch along the sides and bottom edge. Trim the seam allowances to ¼". ⑥

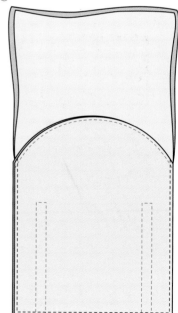

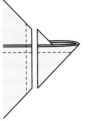
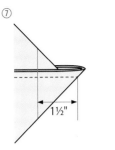

1½"

2. To box the corners, open up the lower-left corner and use your fingers to push it into a triangular point, aligning the side and bottom seams. Draw a line 1½" from the point and perpendicular to the seams. Stitch along the line. Trim the seam allowances to ¼". ⑦

A Perfect Match

To be sure the seams align, push a pin into the side seam so that it exits through the bottom seam.

3. Repeat step 2 to box the lower-right corner.

4. Repeat steps 1–3 with the lining front and back, using a ⅝" seam allowance and leaving a 6" opening in the bottom seam for turning. Trim the seam allowances to ¼".

Lining Smarter

Using a slightly wider seam allowance for the lining than the exterior will ensure a better fit in the finished bag.

5. Turn the bag right side out through the opening in the lining. Press the seam allowances to the wrong side along the opening and machine stitch the opening closed or slip-stitch by hand. Press the bag well for a nicely finished look.

A color variation of the Lucky Denver Mint Bag

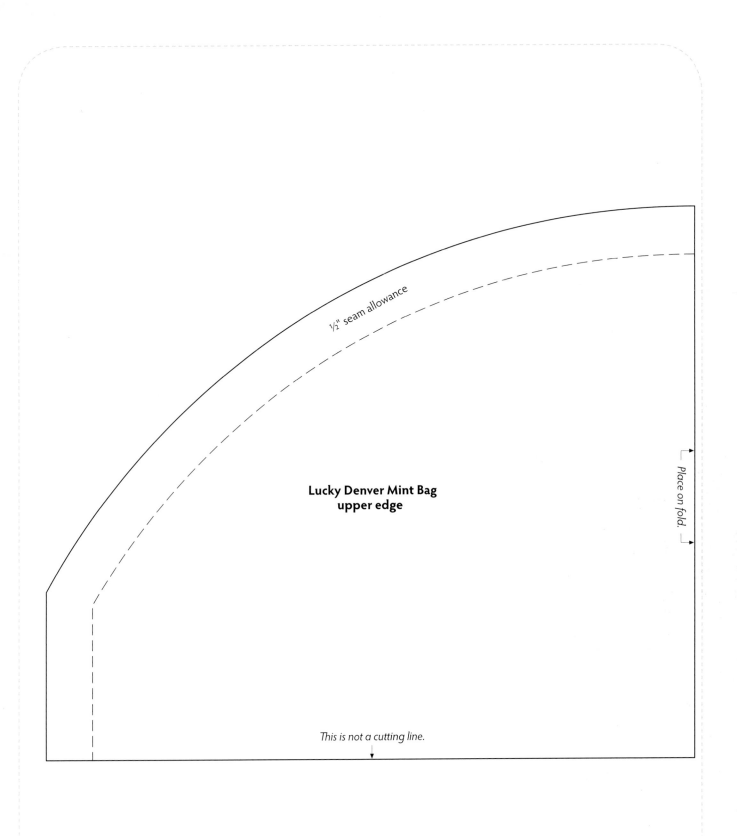

½" seam allowance

**Lucky Denver Mint Bag
upper edge**

Place on fold.

This is not a cutting line.

CHANDELIER SWING BAG

FINISHED BAG: 11" x 7½"

This small, delicate bag is the perfect compliment to your evening wear. It has a recessed zipper and stiff upper body, plus narrow removable straps to make it that much sweeter.

Materials

Yardage is based on 42"-wide fabric.

1 fat quarter of green-and-yellow print for bag exterior
¼ yard of green solid for top panel and strap
⅜ yard of green print for lining
1½ yards of Shape-Flex fusible woven interfacing
¼ yard of Thermolam Plus fusible fleece
¼ yard of Décor Bond fusible interfacing
1 zipper, 12" long
1 zipper, 8" long
2 metal swivel clips (½" opening)
2 metal D-rings (½")

Cutting

The pattern for the top panel is on page 68.

From the green-and-yellow print, cut:
1 rectangle, 6½" x 13", for exterior front
1 rectangle, 6½" x 12", for exterior back
1 rectangle, 2" x 11", for exterior bottom

From the green solid, cut:
1 strip, 1½" x 42", for strap
2 rectangles, 1½" x 2", for strap extenders
4 top panels, *on fold*
2 rectangles, 3" x 1½", for zipper tabs

From the green print, cut:
2 rectangles, 6¼" x 12", for lining front and back
1 rectangle, 9" x 11", for pocket
1 rectangle, 2" x 11", for lining bottom

From the Thermolam Plus, cut:
1 rectangle, 6½" x 13", for exterior front
1 rectangle, 6½" x 12", for exterior back

From the Shape-Flex, cut:
2 rectangles, 6¼" x 12", for lining front and back
1 rectangle, 9" x 11", for pocket
1 rectangle, 1½" x 42", for strap
2 rectangles, 1½" x 2", for strap extenders
2 rectangles, 2" x 11", for exterior and lining bottoms
4 top panels, *on fold*

From the Décor Bond, cut:
8 top panels, *on fold; trim ½" from all edges*
2 rectangles, 1" x 10", for exterior and lining bottoms

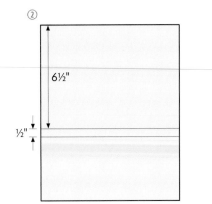

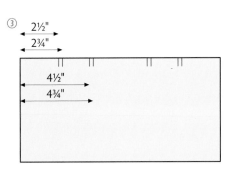

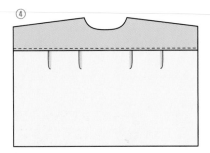

Fuse the Fabrics and Interfacings

1. Fuse the Thermolam Plus pieces to the wrong side of the corresponding fabric pieces for the exterior front and back.

2. Fuse the Shape-Flex pieces to the wrong side of the corresponding pieces for the lining front and back, pocket, strap, strap extenders, exterior bottom, lining bottom, and top panels.

3. Center a Décor Bond top panel on the interfaced side of one fabric top panel and fuse. Repeat to fuse a second layer of Décor Bond to the same top panel. Fuse two layers of Décor Bond to each of the remaining top panel pieces in the same way. Center a rectangle of Décor Bond on the wrong side of each piece for the exterior and lining bottoms and fuse.

Make the Strap

All seam allowances are ½" unless otherwise noted.

1. Fold the strap in half lengthwise with wrong sides together and press. Open the strap and fold both long edges in to meet at the crease; press. Refold along the original crease and press once more. Edgestitch ⅛" from the open long edge to close the strap; do not stitch along the original crease.

2. Prepare the strap extenders in the same way. Edgestitch both long edges of the strap extenders.

3. Press ½" to the wrong side on each short end of the strap. Press an additional 1" to the wrong side on each end.

4. Slide a swivel clip onto each end of the strap, nestling it into the second crease. Sew a small rectangle on each end, securing the folds to the strap. ①

Make the Pocket

1. On the wrong side of the pocket, measure and mark a line 6½" below the short upper edge. Draw another line ½" below the first. ②

2. Continue marking the pocket as directed in "Method 2" of "Zippered Pocket" on page 15.

3. Place the pocket on the exterior back, with the pocket's lower edge 1" above the raw edge of the exterior back and the pocket's left side 1¾" from the side of the exterior back. Pin in place. Using the 8" zipper, continue installing the zippered pocket as directed in "Method 2."

Assemble the Exterior

1. Measuring from the left edge and using a removable marker, make four marks across the upper 13"-long edge of the exterior front. Space the marks 2½", 2¾", 4½", and 4¾" from the left edge. ③

2. To form pleats, fold the bag wrong sides together along the first mark and bring the first mark to meet the second. Press the pleat at the upper edge and pin it in place. Make a second pleat by folding along the third mark and matching it to the fourth mark; press and pin.

3. Repeat steps 1 and 2, measuring from the right edge, to make a second set of marks and pleats along the upper edge.

4. Baste across the pleats, stitching ¼" from the bag's upper edge.

5. Place the pleated exterior front and one top panel, right sides together, matching the pleated edge of the exterior front to the long straight edge of the top panel. Stitch and then press the seam allowances toward the top panel.

6. Edgestitch the top panel ⅛" above the seam. ④

7. Stitch the exterior back to a second top panel in the same way, omitting the pleats.

8. Sew the exterior front and back together along the side edges, using a ¼" seam allowance. Press the seam allowances open.

9. Mark the bottom raw edges of the exterior front and back ¾" from each side seam. Make a ⅜"-long clip at each mark.

10. Pin the bag bottom to the bag, matching the raw edges. Center each exterior side seam along one short end of the exterior bottom. The seam allowance will open to fit around the corners at each clip.

11. Sew the exterior bottom to the bag, pivoting at each corner. Trim the bottom corners diagonally, being careful not to cut into the stitches. Turn the bag right side out and press.

Assemble the Top Panels

1. Press one zipper tab in half widthwise with wrong sides together, making a 1½" square. Open the fabric and press opposite edges to meet at the center crease. Refold along the original crease and press once more to make a tiny strip of double-fold tape. Repeat with the remaining zipper tab.

2. Trim the zipper tape to measure exactly ¾" from the upper zipper stops. Slip the top of the zipper into the center fold of one zipper tab; the folds should rest just above the upper stops. Stitch ⅛" from the fabric folds through all the layers, taking care not to hit the zipper stops. Lay the zipper on a top panel and trim the bottom of the zipper to match the panel's width, if necessary. It is OK to cut off the lower zipper stop while the zipper is closed. Slip the bottom of the zipper into the second zipper tab and edgestitch as before. ⑤

3. Trim the zipper tabs to match the width of the zipper tapes. Trim ¼" from the bottom edge of the remaining top panel.

4. Fold one prepared strap extender in half around a metal D-ring, matching the raw edges. Position the strap extender on the straight edge of one top panel, 1" from the panel's right edge, on the right side of

A color variation of the Chandelier Swing Bag

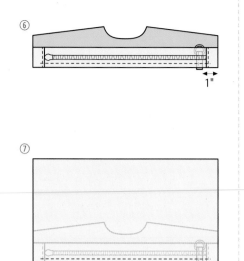

⑥

the panel. Place the zipper right side down on the panel, sandwiching the strap extender between the layers. Align the edges and pin. With a zipper foot, sew the zipper to the panel with a ¼" seam allowance, beginning and ending the seam ½" from the panel's side edges. The strap extender will be caught in the seam. ⑥

5. Place the lining front on the top panel unit, right sides together, with the zipper sandwiched between the fabric layers. Sew directly on top of the previous stitches. ⑦

6. Turn the unit right side out and press. Edgestitch the top panel ⅛" from the zipper tape. Sew from one end of the zipper to the other, but do not sew across the zipper tabs.

7. Repeat steps 4–6 to attach the other side of the zipper to the lining back and the remaining top panel. Remove the zipper foot from your machine.

Finish the Bag

1. Unzip the zipper. Sew the lining front and back together at the side seams. Refer to "Assemble the Exterior," steps 9–11 on page 67, to stitch the lining bottom to the lining, leaving a 6" opening along one long edge.

2. Slip the lining over the bag exterior with right sides together. Pin in place, matching the side seams.

3. Sew the entire top edge of the bag using a ¼" seam allowance. Clip the seam allowances along the curved edges, being careful not to cut into the stitches.

4. Turn the bag right side out through the opening in the lining. Press the top edge and edgestitch it ⅛" from the seam.

5. Press the seam allowances to the wrong side along the opening in the lining. Machine stitch the opening closed or slip-stitch it by hand.

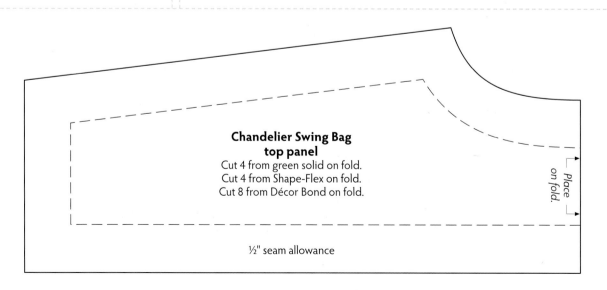

**Chandelier Swing Bag
top panel**
Cut 4 from green solid on fold.
Cut 4 from Shape-Flex on fold.
Cut 8 from Décor Bond on fold.

½" seam allowance

Place on fold.

MISS INDEPENDENT BAG

FINISHED BAG: 16½" x 11¾" • LAPTOP CASE: 15" x 11¾"
This bag is perfect to sling over your shoulder for work or school. There's room for file folders, books, and all your personal items. The padded laptop case will fit many models of computers and tablets, 13" or smaller. This is one sturdy bag, perfect for your busy day-to-day life!

Materials

Yardage is based on 42"-wide fabric. Supplies are listed separately for the bag and laptop case.

FOR THE BAG

1 yard of gray print for exterior
1 yard of polka-dot fabric for lining
1 yard of Deco-Fuse fusible interfacing
2¼ yards of Shape-Flex fusible woven interfacing
1 yard of Thermolam Plus fusible fleece
1 package of ½"-wide double-fold bias tape (or make 2 yards of your own)
1 pair of 28" leather handles with prepunched tabs
2 magnetic snaps (½")
1 zipper, 7" long
1 separating zipper, 14" long
Tapestry or heavyweight thread*

*Or use double- or triple-strand of regular thread

FOR THE LAPTOP CASE

½ yard of white print for exterior
½ yard of polka-dot fabric for lining
¾ yard of Thermolam Plus fusible fleece
1 zipper, 16" long

Cutting

Follow the cutting instructions for each project individually. If you're using the same fabrics for both projects, cut the largest pieces first to conserve fabric. I used a laminated canvas for the bag exterior.

FOR THE BAG

The patterns for the large and small flaps are on page 76.

From the gray print, cut:
2 rectangles, 12¼" x 18¼", for exterior front and back*
1 rectangle, 5½" x 18¼", for exterior bottom
2 rectangles, 5½" x 12", for exterior sides
2 rectangles, 2" x 16½", for exterior zipper panels
1 small flap, *on fold*
1 large flap, *on fold*
1 rectangle, 6" x 7", for exterior small pocket
1 rectangle, 7" x 9", for exterior large pocket
1 rectangle, 2" x 18", for exterior small pocket panel
1 rectangle, 2" x 20½", for exterior large pocket panel

From the polka-dot fabric, cut:
2 rectangles, 12¼" x 18¼", for lining front and back*
1 rectangle, 5½" x 18¼", for lining bottom
2 rectangles, 5½" x 12", for lining sides
2 rectangles, 2" x 16½", for lining zipper panels
1 small flap, *on fold*
1 large flap, *on fold*
1 rectangle, 6" x 7", for lining small pocket
1 rectangle, 7" x 9", for lining large pocket
1 rectangle, 2" x 18", for lining small pocket panel
1 rectangle, 2" x 20½", for lining large pocket panel
1 rectangle, 8" x 12", for interior pocket

Continued on page 71

"Cutting" continued from page 69

From the Deco-Fuse, cut:
2 rectangles, 12¼" x 18¼", for exterior front and back*
1 rectangle, 4½" x 17", for exterior bottom

From the Shape-Flex, cut:
2 rectangles, 12¼" x 18¼", for lining front and back*
1 rectangle, 5½" x 18¼", for lining bottom
2 rectangles, 5½" x 12", for lining side panels
2 rectangles, 2" x 16½", for lining zipper panels
2 rectangles, 2" x 16½", for exterior zipper panels
1 small flap, *on fold*
1 large flap, *on fold*
1 rectangle, 6" x 7", for small pocket
1 rectangle, 7" x 9", for large pocket
1 rectangle, 2" x 18", for small pocket panel
1 rectangle, 2" x 20½", for large pocket panel
1 rectangle, 8" x 12", for interior pocket

From the Thermolam Plus, cut:
2 rectangles, 12¼" x 18¼", for front and back*
1 rectangle, 5½" x 18¼", for bottom
2 rectangles, 5½" x 12", for sides
4 rectangles, 2" x 16½", for exterior and lining zipper panels
1 small flap, *on fold*
1 large flap, *on fold*
1 rectangle, 6" x 7", for small pocket
1 rectangle, 7" x 9", for large pocket
1 rectangle, 2" x 18", for small pocket panel
1 rectangle, 2" x 20½", for large pocket panel
2 squares, 1½" x 1½", for reinforcement

*After cutting the rectangles, refer to "Working with the Pattern" at right to curve the upper corners.

FOR THE LAPTOP CASE

From the white print, cut:
2 rectangles, 13¼" x 17¼", for exterior front and back
2 rectangles, 1½" x 3", for zipper tabs

From the polka-dot fabric, cut:
2 rectangles, 13¼" x 17¼", for lining front and back

From the Thermolam Plus, cut:
4 rectangles, 12" x 16¼"

To create each main panel, begin with a 12¼" x 18" fabric rectangle. Fold the rectangle in half so that it measures 12¼" x 9", and position the fold on the left.

Trace the upper edge pattern on page 77 onto paper or cardstock to make a template. Mark the edge that will be placed on the fabric fold.

Place the template on the folded fabric, aligning the upper-left corners. Trace the template to shape the upper-right corner and the upper part of the right edge. Remove the template and draw a line connecting the bottom of the traced outline to the lower-right corner of the folded fabric. Cut along the lines to shape the main panel; make two each of exterior fabric, lining, Deco-Fuse, Shape-Flex, and Thermolam Plus.

Open the folds and trim ½" from all four sides of the Deco-Fuse pieces.

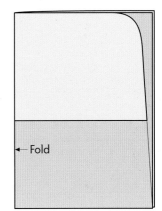

← Fold

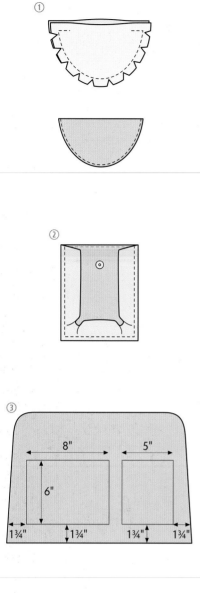

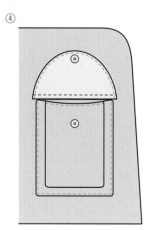

Fuse the Fabrics and Interfacings (Both Projects)

1. Center the Deco-Fuse pieces on the wrong side of the corresponding gray front, back, and bottom pieces, and fuse in place.

2. Fuse the Shape-Flex pieces to the wrong side of the corresponding fabric pieces for the lining sides, front, back, and bottom; exterior and lining zipper panels; small and large pockets and pocket panels; and interior pocket. Fuse the Shape-Flex to the wrong side of the small and large gray flaps.

3. Fuse the Thermolam Plus pieces to the wrong side of the corresponding pieces for the exterior front, back, sides, and bottom; exterior and lining zipper panels; small and large pockets and panels; and small and large lining flaps.

4. Trace a drinking glass or other round object on each lower corner of the prepared exterior and lining side pieces. Cut along the lines to curve the lower corners.

5. Center a piece of Thermolam Plus on the wrong side of each laptop case exterior and lining rectangle and fuse.

Attach the Snaps

1. Mark the snap positions at the center of each small and large lining flap, 1" above the curved edges.

2. Install the thinner half of a magnetic snap at each placement mark, referring to "Magnetic Snaps" on page 16. Use the 1½" squares of Thermolam Plus to reinforce the snaps.

3. Mark the snap placement on the small pocket, centered 1¾" below the 6" upper edge of the pocket. Mark the placement on the large pocket, centered 1¾" below the 9" upper edge. Install the thicker half of a magnetic snap at each placement mark.

Make the Front Pockets

All seam allowances are ½" unless otherwise noted.

1. With right sides together, sew the small pocket to the corresponding lining piece around all four edges, leaving a 4" opening at the center of the upper edge and pivoting at each corner. Trim the corners diagonally to reduce bulk.

2. Turn the pocket right side out through the opening. Fold the raw edges to the wrong side along the opening and press the pocket well. Edgestitch ⅛" from the upper edge, closing the opening.

Something Shiny

I used laminated canvas for the sample bag. You may need to adjust your sewing techniques and eliminate the edgestitching on the flaps.

3. Repeat steps 1 and 2 with the large pocket and its lining.

4. Assemble the small and large flaps the same way, leaving an opening along the straight edge of each. Before turning, notch the seam allowances along the curved edges, being careful not to cut into the stitches. *Optional:* edgestitch the curved flap edges, but do not stitch the straight edges at this time. ①

5. Assemble each pocket panel in the same way, leaving an opening along one long edge. Do not edgestitch; leave the opening unsewn for now.

6. Pin the small pocket panel to the small pocket sides and lower edge, matching the upper edges. Place the pieces right sides together, with the opening in the panel against the pocket edge. Sew with a ¼" seam allowance, closing the opening in the panel as you stitch. Press the seam allowances toward the pocket. Assemble the large pocket in the same way. ②

Directional Sewing

I recommend sewing both sides of the pocket to the panel first, working from the upper edge toward the lower corners. It's easier to distribute the panel's fullness evenly with this technique.

7. With a removable marker, make a mark on the right side of the exterior front 1¾" above the lower edge and 1¾" from the right edge. Starting at this point, draw a rectangle 5" wide and 6" high. Pin the assembled small pocket to the guidelines along the sides and bottom with right sides out, leaving the top edge open.

8. Edgestitch the pocket panel to the bag, ⅛" from the panel edges. When finished, the pocket will stand away from the bag front.

9. Repeat steps 7 and 8 to attach the large pocket, working from the left edge of the bag and drawing a rectangle 8" wide and 6" high. ③

10. Pin the small flap at the top of the small pocket with the flap and bag right sides together. Position the flap's straight edge on the top line of the placement rectangle. Fold the pinned flap over the pocket and snap the closure; be sure the flap appears straight and make any necessary adjustments before sewing. Unsnap and stitch the flap to the bag ¼" from the flap's straight edge. Repeat to attach the large flap over the large pocket. ④

Make the Lining Pocket

Mark the lining back with a rectangle, 4" below the upper edge and centered from side to side, referring to "Zippered Pocket" on page 14. Insert the interior pocket, using the 7" zipper.

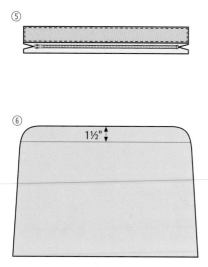

⑤

⑥

⑦

Attach the Zipper

1. Press ¼" to the wrong side along one long and both short edges of both zipper panels and the two lining zipper panels.

2. Place the separating zipper along the unpressed 16" edge of one zipper panel, right sides together, centering the zipper on the zipper panel. Pin in place. With a zipper foot, sew the zipper to the panel, using a ¼" seam allowance.

3. Align the raw edge of one lining zipper panel with the zipper edge of the assembled unit and pin. Sew directly on top of the previous stitches.

4. Turn the assembled unit right side out and press. Edgestitch ⅛" from the zipper seam and the pressed edges, beginning at one short end and pivoting at each corner, to completely enclose the raw edges. ⑤

5. Attach the remaining zipper panel and lining zipper panel to the other side of the zipper in the same way.

6. Draw a line 1½" below the top of the lining front on the right side of the fabric, using a removable marker. ⑥

7. Align one long edge of the zipper unit with the line, right side down, with the zipper unit toward the top of the lining front. Position the short ends of the zipper unit ½" from each side of the lining front. Pin and sew the zipper unit in place on top of the previous stitches along the long edge of the zipper unit. ⑦

8. Unzip the zipper, and then repeat steps 6 and 7 to attach the other side of the zipper unit to the lining back.

Assemble the Bag

1. Mark handle-tab placements on the exterior front and back, 3" below the upper edge and 3" from the side edges. Referring to "Leather Handles" on page 19, hand sew each tab in place.

2. Sew the exterior front and back to the long edges of the exterior bottom. Press the seam allowances open. Repeat with the lining pieces. Lay the assembled lining on the exterior, wrong sides together and raw edges matched, and pin.

3. Sew a side panel to a lining side panel along the short, straight upper edge. Press the seam allowances open, and then align the pieces with wrong sides together and press again. Topstitch ¼" from the stitched edge. Make two.

4. Fold the exterior bottom and each side panel to find the centers of the short edges that meet at the bottom. Pin the exterior sides to the bag, wrong sides together, matching the center marks. Position the top-stitched edge of each side panel just below the zipper panel. Baste ⅜" from the raw edges.

5. Open out the bias tape and position it on the bag, right sides together, matching the raw edges. Begin sewing ½" from the end of the tape

⑧

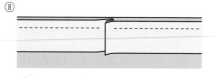

⑨

in an unobtrusive part of the bag, near the exterior bottom. Sew along the first crease in the binding, attaching the bias tape to the bag. Continue around the entire bag edge. When you return to the beginning, trim the excess bias tape, leaving a 1" overlap. Press ½" to the wrong side and slip it under the beginning of the bias tape. Finish sewing the bias tape to the bag. ⑧

6. Fold the bias tape over the edge of the bag to the lining side. To finish the inside edge of the binding, either topstitch by machine or slip-stitch by hand.

Handy Tip

Maneuvering a sewing-machine needle through some areas of the bag may be tricky. Feel free to hand stitch any difficult parts of the bias trim. I found that slip-stitching the interior edge of the binding by hand yields a neater finish.

Make the Laptop Case

All seam allowances are ½" unless otherwise noted.

1. Referring to "Top Zip" on page 12, prepare and attach the zipper to the laptop case front and back, and add the lining pieces.

2. Open the zipper at least halfway. Open out the assembled pieces to align the lining pieces, right sides together, on one side of the zipper, and the bag pieces, right sides together, on the other side of the zipper. Pin the raw edges. Starting at one end of the zipper, sew the bag exterior pieces together along the sides and bottom edge, pivoting at each corner and finishing at the other end of the zipper. Do not sew across the zipper tabs.

3. Repeat to join the lining fabrics, using a ⅝" seam allowance and leaving a 6" opening along the bottom for turning.

Seams Smart

Using a slightly wider seam allowance for the lining than the exterior will ensure a better fit in the finished bag.

4. Fold one lower corner of the bag exterior to form a triangle, aligning the side and bottom seams. Draw a line perpendicular to the seam lines and 1" from the point. ⑨

Seamly Alignment

To align the seams, push a pin into the side seam so that it exits through the bottom seam.

Two color variations of the Miss Independent Bag

5. Stitch along the line. Trim the corner, leaving a ¼" seam allowance. Box the other lower corner of the case and both of the case lining's lower corners in the same way.

6. Turn the case right side out through the opening in the lining. Press the seam allowances to the wrong side along the opening and either top-stitch the opening closed by machine or slip-stitch it by hand.

7. Tuck the lining inside the laptop case. Press the case well for a nicely finished look.

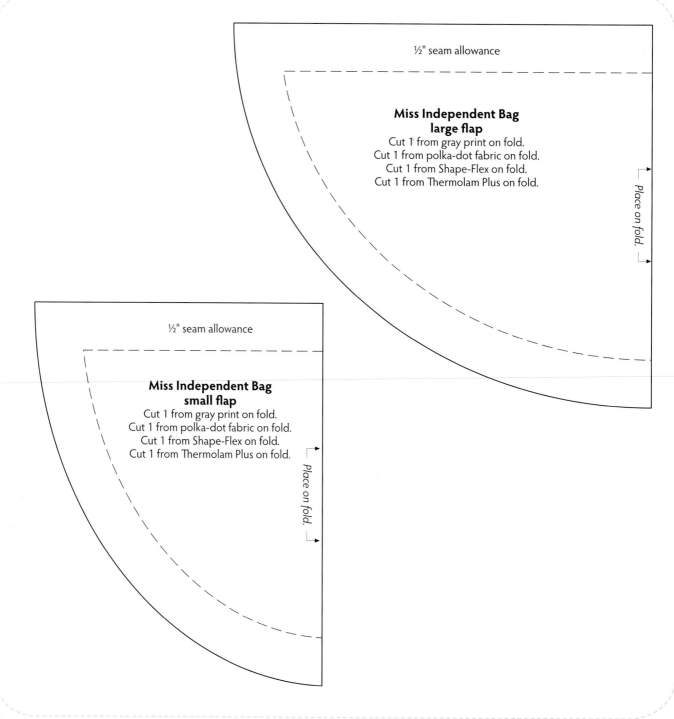

½" seam allowance

**Miss Independent Bag
large flap**
Cut 1 from gray print on fold.
Cut 1 from polka-dot fabric on fold.
Cut 1 from Shape-Flex on fold.
Cut 1 from Thermolam Plus on fold.

Place on fold.

½" seam allowance

**Miss Independent Bag
small flap**
Cut 1 from gray print on fold.
Cut 1 from polka-dot fabric on fold.
Cut 1 from Shape-Flex on fold.
Cut 1 from Thermolam Plus on fold.

Place on fold.

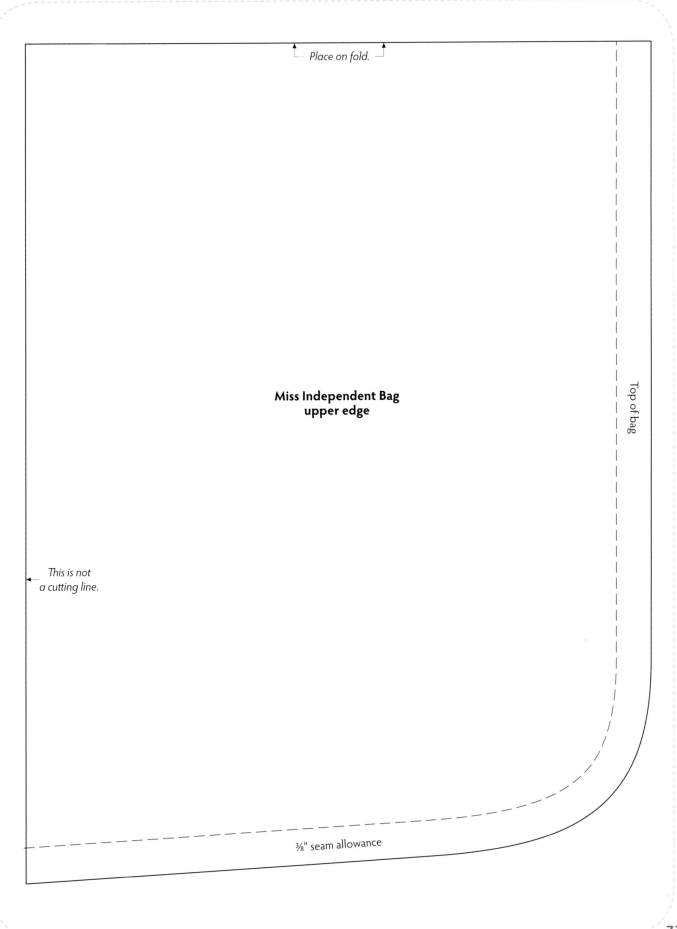

Place on fold.

Miss Independent Bag
upper edge

Top of bag

This is not
a cutting line.

⅜" seam allowance

HONEYMOONER SUITCASE

FINISHED BAG: 18" x 12½" x 5"

Escape the daily grind and run away on a mini vacation with this small yet style-packed suitcase. You can pack a few days' worth of outfits into this little gem. The piped edges provide a professional finish, and you can give it your own burst of style with a pretty handle and great home-decor fabric.

Materials

Yardage is based on 54"-wide home-decor–weight fabric.

¾ yard of green print for exterior

¾ yard of light-green solid for lining

1½ yards of Thermolam Plus fusible fleece

1½ yards of Shape-Flex fusible woven interfacing

1 yard of Deco-Fuse fusible inter-facing (or substitute Peltex One-Sided Fusible)

3 packages (3 yards each) of ½"-wide double-fold bias tape

3½ yards of ⁸/₃₂" cotton cording

1 sport zipper, 48" long

2 metal rectangle rings (1½")

Optional: piping foot and jeans/ denim needle

Cutting

From the green print, cut:
1 rectangle, 6" x 48", for exterior side panel
2 rectangles, 13½" x 19", for exterior front and back
1 rectangle, 5" x 10¾", for exterior top panel
2 rectangles, 1½" x 3", for zipper tabs
2 rectangles, 2½" x 8", for handles
4 rectangles, 2½" x 9", for handle sides

From the light-green solid, cut:
1 rectangle, 6" x 48", for lining side panel
2 rectangles, 13½" x 19", for lining front and back
1 rectangle, 5" x 10¾", for lining top panel

From the Thermolam Plus, cut:
1 rectangle, 6" x 48", for exterior side panel
2 rectangles, 13½" x 19", for exterior front and back
1 rectangle, 5" x 10¾", for exterior top panel
3 rectangles, 1¼" x 5", for handle

From the Shape-Flex, cut:
1 rectangle, 6" x 48", for lining side panel
2 rectangles, 13½" x 19", for lining front and back
1 rectangle, 5" x 10¾", for lining top panel
2 rectangles, 2½" x 8", for handles
4 rectangles, 2½" x 9", for handle sides

From the Deco-Fuse, cut:
2 rectangles, 12½" x 18", for exterior front and back

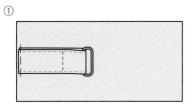

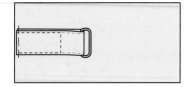

Fuse the Fabrics and Interfacings

1. Trace a drinking glass or other curved item to round all four corners of the exterior and lining fronts and backs. Trim along the marked curves. Mark and trim the corresponding pieces of Deco-Fuse, Thermolam Plus, and Shape-Flex to match.

2. Fuse the Thermolam Plus pieces to the wrong side of the corresponding fabric pieces for the exterior side, front, back, and top panel.

3. Center the Deco-Fuse pieces on the interfaced side of the exterior front and back and fuse in place.

4. Fuse the Shape-Flex pieces to the wrong side of the corresponding pieces for the lining side, front, back, and top, as well as the handles and handle sides.

Make the Handle

All seam allowances are ½" unless otherwise noted.

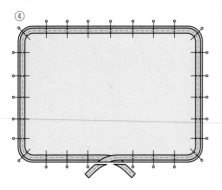

1. Sew two handle sides, right sides together, along both long edges. Turn right side out and press. Edgestitch ⅛" from the finished edges. Make two.

2. Fold an assembled handle side in half around a rectangle ring, matching the raw edges. Make two.

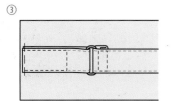

3. Center a folded handle side on one short end of the top panel, matching the raw edges. Baste ¼" from the raw edges. Repeat to baste the second handle side to the other short end of the top panel. Topstitch across each handle side, 3" from the nearest raw edges. ①

4. To further reinforce the handle sides, stitch along the previous stitches from the raw edge to the 3" line; pivot and sew across the handle sides; and pivot once more to sew back to the raw edges. ②

5. Center a 1¼" x 5" piece of Thermolam Plus on the wrong side of one handle piece and fuse. Add the two remaining pieces of Thermolam Plus, one at a time, fusing them directly on top of the first to make a thick stack.

6. Sew the handle pieces, right sides together, along both long edges. Turn right side out and press. Edgestitch ⅛" from each finished edge.

7. Press ½" to the wrong side of each short end of the assembled handle. Press an additional 1" to the wrong side on each end.

8. Slide a rectangle ring onto each end of the handle, nestling it into the second crease. Sew a small rectangle through the hem on each end, enclosing the first pressed edges. ③

Attach the Zipper

1. Prepare the zipper tabs and zipper, referring to "Top Zip" on page 12. If necessary, trim the zipper tape to exactly 48"; do not remove the zipper stops or zipper pull.

2. Cut the exterior and lining side panels in half, lengthwise, to yield two 3" x 48" strips of each. Install the zipper as directed in "Top Zip."

3. Sew the exterior side panel to the exterior top panel, right sides together, along one short edge. Move the side panel lining out of the way so it is not caught in the seam. Repeat to sew the remaining short edges of the exterior side and top panels together.

4. Repeat step 3 to sew the short ends of the lining side and top panels together.

Attach the Piping

1. Cut a 25" segment of bias tape from one packaged length and join it to the full length of a second package. Press the seam allowances open.

2. Press the joined bias tape to remove the top and bottom creases, leaving the center crease intact. Trim the tape ⅝" from the fold for a total width of 1¼". Fold the bias tape around the cording, nestling the cording in the crease.

3. Using the zipper foot, stitch ¼" from the raw edges of the bias tape, securing the cording in the fold. Divide the piping into two equal lengths and sew across all four ends to secure the cording.

4. Pin one length of piping to the exterior front, beginning at the center of the bottom edge and tapering the end of the piping into the seam allowance. Ease the cording at the corner curves and pin around the entire edge of the exterior front, matching the raw edges. When the end meets the beginning at the center bottom, taper the piping into the seam allowance and trim any excess piping. ④

5. Sew the piping to the exterior front on top of the previous stitches. Clip the seam allowances along the curves of the exterior front and piping, being careful not to cut into the stitches.

6. Repeat steps 4 and 5 to baste the second length of piping to the exterior back.

Assemble the Bag

1. Place the front lining on the exterior front, wrong sides together, and baste ¼" from the raw edges. Fold the unit at each curved corner and mark the center of each curve with a pin. Repeat to baste and mark the exterior back to its lining. Baste and mark the exterior and lining side/top panels together in the same way.

⑤

2. Center the assembled bag top on the upper raw edge of the bag front, right sides together. The seams enclosing the handle ends should lie 4½" from the side edges of the exterior front. Pin the top/side panel to the entire edge of the exterior front, easing around the corners. Sew, using a zipper or piping foot to stitch as close to the cording as possible. If it's not possible to feel the cording through all the layers of interfacing, measure and mark the seam line before sewing. Press the seam allowances toward the front panel.

Getting the Point

I recommend using a denim or jeans needle to sew through the multiple layers of home-decor fabric and piping. These needles have a true sharp point that pierces the fabric weave easily.

3. Attach the free edge of the side/top panel to the exterior back in the same way. Be sure the marked corners of the front and back align across the side panel to avoid skewing the bag. ⑤

4. Notch the seam allowances along the curved corners, being careful not to cut into the stitches.

5. Sew the remaining lengths of bias tape together along one short edge. Press the seam open. Press ½" to the wrong side along one short end of the bias tape.

6. Open the bias tape to expose the creases. With the bag lining side out, pin one long raw edge of the binding to the seam allowances along the exterior back, matching the raw edges. Begin pinning at the center of the bottom edge with the pressed end of the bias tape. Ease the bias tape around the curved corners of the bag. When you return to the pressed leading edge of the bias, trim the excess bias tape, leaving a ½" overlap; this will enclose the raw edge of the tape.

7. Sew along the first crease in the bias tape through all layers. Fold the bias tape over the seam allowances to the side/top panel and refold the bias along the pressed creases. Pin in place. Topstitch ¼" from the outer edge of the bias tape to secure it over the seam allowances, or slip-stitch the fold by hand.

8. Press ½" to the wrong side on one short end of the remaining bias tape. Repeat steps 6 and 7 to bind the bag front panel seam allowances.

PICCADILLY CIRCUS HANDBAG

FINISHED BAG: 15" x 8" x 5"

This small yet stylish bag is perfect for tucking under your arm. The zippered top will keep all your carry-along items safe, while the solid-color accents and the handles' metal rings provide nice finishing touches.

Materials

Yardage is based on 42"-wide fabric.

⅝ yard of multicolored print for exterior

⅝ yard of turquoise print for accents and handles

¾ yard of blue print for lining

1⅝ yards of Shape-Flex fusible woven interfacing

1 yard of Thermolam Plus fusible fleece

½ yard of Décor Bond fusible interfacing

4 metal O-rings (1½")

1 zipper, 24" long

Cutting

The patterns for the side panel, accent piece, and handle tab are on page 88.

From the multicolored print, cut:
2 rectangles, 9" x 16", for exterior front and back
1 rectangle, 5" x 26", for exterior zipper panel

From the turquoise print, cut:
2 rectangles, 4" x 22", for handles
1 rectangle, 6" x 16", for exterior bottom
2 side panels, *on fold*
4 accent pieces
8 handle tabs, *on fold*

From the blue print, cut:
2 rectangles, 9" x 16", for lining front and back
1 rectangle, 5" x 26", for lining zipper panel
1 rectangle, 6" x 16", for lining bottom
2 rectangles, 10" x 14", for pockets
2 side panels, *on fold*

From the Shape-Flex, cut:
2 rectangles, 4" x 22", for handles
2 rectangles, 6" x 16", for bottoms
2 rectangles, 10" x 14", for pockets
4 accent pieces
8 handle tabs, *on fold*

From the Thermolam Plus, cut:
4 rectangles, 9" x 16", for fronts and backs
2 rectangles, 5" x 26", for zipper panels
4 side panels, *on fold*

From the Décor Bond, cut:
2 rectangles, 5" x 15", for bottoms

Fuse the Fabrics and Interfacings

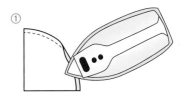

1. Fuse the Thermolam Plus pieces to the wrong side of the corresponding fabric pieces for the exterior and lining fronts, backs, sides, and zipper panels.

2. Fuse the Shape-Flex pieces to the wrong side of the corresponding pieces for the handles, handle tabs, accents, pockets, and exterior and lining bottoms.

3. Center a piece of Décor Bond on the wrong side of each interfaced bottom piece and fuse in place.

Attach the Accent Pieces and Handle Tabs

All seam allowances are ½" unless otherwise noted.

1. Sew ¼" from the curved edge of each accent piece.

2. Press the curved edge to the wrong side along the stitching, easing the fabric to fit. Make four. ①

3. Place a prepared accent on each lower corner of the exterior front, matching the raw edges. Edgestitch ⅛" from the pressed edges. Continue stitching ⅛" from the raw edges to baste the accents in place. Repeat to stitch the remaining accent pieces to the exterior back. ②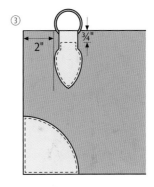

4. Sew two handle tabs right sides together with a ¼" seam allowance, leaving the straight edge open. Notch the seam allowances along the curved edge and clip into the corners, being careful not to cut into the stitches. Turn the tabs right side out and press. Make four.

5. Fold and press 2" of each tab's straight edge to the wrong side. Slide one metal O-ring into the crease of each handle tab.

6. With a removable marker, draw vertical lines 2" from each side edge of the exterior front and back. Position one handle tab along each line as shown, aligning the ring crease of the tab with the bag's upper raw edge. Pin in place. Draw a horizontal line on each handle tab, ¾" below the ring crease.

7. Topstitch along the ¾" line on each handle tab, continuing to stitch ⅛" from the curved edge around the lower portion of the tab. Pivot the stitching at the corners and lower point. ③

Make and Attach the Handles

1. Press ½" to the wrong side along each long edge of one handle piece.

2. Press the handle in half lengthwise, enclosing the long raw edges. Edgestitch ⅛" from both long edges.

3. Fold one short end of the handle to the wrong side ½" and press. Fold an additional 1" to the wrong side and press again. Repeat on the opposite short end of the handle.

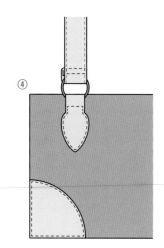

4. Slide the prepared handle through the ring on the left side of the exterior front, positioning the ring in the handle's second pressed crease. Sew a small rectangle through the handle, enclosing the raw edges. Attach the free end of the handle to the ring on the right side of the exterior front in the same way. Be sure the strap is not twisted. ④

5. Repeat steps 1–4 to make the second handle and attach it to the exterior back.

Make the Zipper Panel

1. Cut the exterior and lining zipper panels in half lengthwise to make two 2½" x 26" rectangles of each fabric.

2. Construct the zipper panel, following the instructions in "Zipper Panel" on page 13.

Make the Pockets

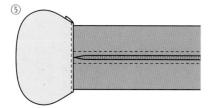

1. Fold one pocket in half, right sides together, to make a 7" x 10" rectangle. Sew along the three raw edges, leaving a 3" opening along one edge for turning.

2. Trim the corners diagonally to reduce bulk. Turn the pocket right side out and press.

3. Topstitch ¼" from the folded edge of the pocket. With the folded edge as the top of the pocket, finger-press the pocket in half to mark the vertical centerline. Fold and mark the lining front centerline in the same way.

4. Place the pocket right side up on the right side of the lining front, with the pocket's lower edge 2" above the lining front's lower edge and the centers aligned. Edgestitch the pocket sides and lower edge ⅛" from the edge, leaving the pocket top open.

5. Repeat steps 1–4 to make the second pocket and attach it to the lining back.

Finish the Bag

1. Using a drinking glass or other round object, trace a curve at each upper corner of the exterior front and back. Trim the pieces along the curved lines.

2. Sew the lower edge of the bag front to the bag bottom. Press the seam allowances toward the bottom.

3. Sew the exterior back to the free edge of the exterior bottom. Press the seam allowances toward the bottom.

4. Sew the side panels to the short ends of the prepared zipper panel. Press the seam allowances toward the side panels and edgestitch the side panels ⅛" from the seam lines. ⑤

5. Unzip the zipper. Pin the assembled bag zipper panel to the bag exterior, right sides together, aligning the upper edges of the side and bag accents. Tuck or pin the handles out of the way. Sew the entire seam. Trim the corners diagonally to reduce bulk and clip the seam allowances along the curves, being careful not to cut into the stitches. Turn right side out and press well.

> **Sew Easy**
> *It may be helpful to sew from the upper edge toward the bottom of the bag when attaching the side pieces. It's easier to distribute the fullness evenly when the bottom edge is sewn last.*

6. Repeat steps 1–5 with the lining pieces. Leave the lining wrong side out.

7. Place the lining inside the bag exterior, wrong sides together. Slip-stitch the pressed edge of the lining along the zipper on the lining side.

A color variation of the Piccadilly Circus Bag

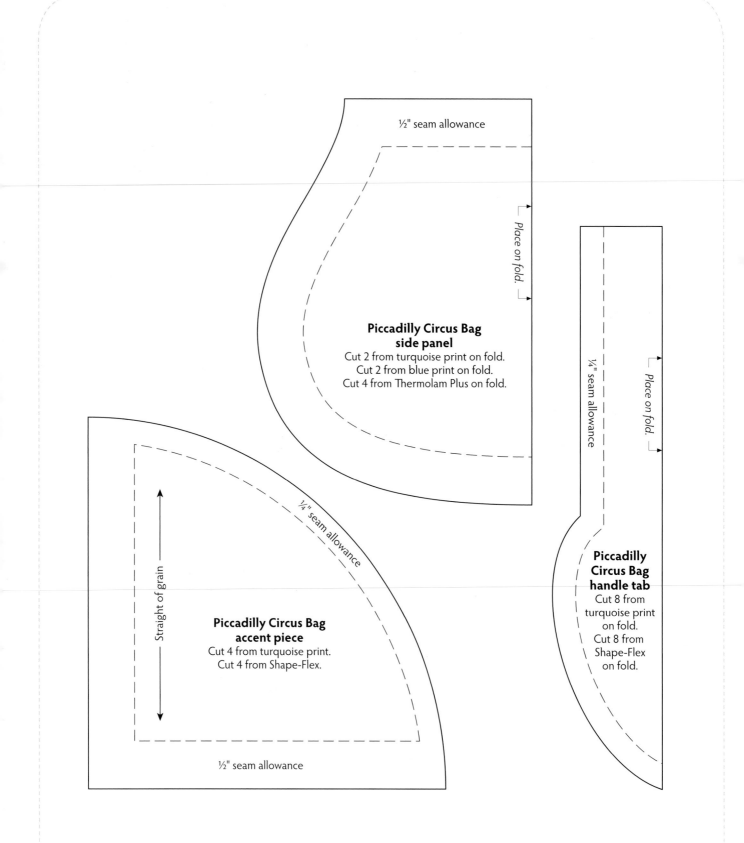

½" seam allowance

Place on fold.

Piccadilly Circus Bag side panel
Cut 2 from turquoise print on fold.
Cut 2 from blue print on fold.
Cut 4 from Thermolam Plus on fold.

¼" seam allowance

Place on fold.

Piccadilly Circus Bag handle tab
Cut 8 from turquoise print on fold.
Cut 8 from Shape-Flex on fold.

¼" seam allowance

Straight of grain

Piccadilly Circus Bag accent piece
Cut 4 from turquoise print.
Cut 4 from Shape-Flex.

½" seam allowance

SOUND CHECK BAG

FINISHED BAG: 19" (at widest point) x 11"

This bag is inspired by my friend Kay Whitt and her Sally Shirtdress sewing pattern for Serendipity Studio. Like the dress, this bag features pretty pleats that are gorgeous, yet very easy to do! The Sound Check Bag is a soft bag with inner pockets and a snap closure, as well as eye-catching knotted straps.

Materials

Yardage is based on 42"-wide fabric.

1 yard of purple print for exterior
1 yard of blue solid for accents and lining
2½ yards of Shape-Flex fusible woven interfacing
½ yard of Thermolam Plus fusible fleece
¼ yard of Décor Bond fusible interfacing
4 metal rectangle rings (1½")
1 magnetic snap (½")

Cutting

From the purple print, cut:
2 rectangles, 4" x 36", for straps
4 rectangles, 2¼" x 4", for strap extenders
2 rectangles, 14½" x 18", for exterior front and back
2 rectangles, 7" x 12", for exterior sides

From the blue solid, cut:
2 rectangles, 14½" x 15", for lining front and back
4 rectangles, 7" x 12", for lining sides and pockets
4 rectangles, 2" x 14½", for accents
1 rectangle, 4" x 21", for exterior bottom

From the Shape-Flex, cut:
2 rectangles, 4" x 36", for straps
4 rectangles, 2¼" x 4", for strap extenders
2 rectangles, 14½" x 18", for exterior front and back
4 rectangles, 7" x 12", for pockets and exterior sides
4 rectangles, 2" x 14½", for accents
1 rectangle, 4" x 21", for exterior bottom

From the Thermolam Plus, cut:
2 rectangles, 14½" x 15", for lining front and back
2 rectangles, 7" x 12", for lining sides

From the Décor Bond, cut:
4 rectangles, 1" x 13½", for accents
1 rectangle, 3" x 20", for exterior bottom

Fuse the Fabrics and Interfacings

1. Fuse the Shape-Flex pieces to the wrong side of the corresponding fabric pieces for the straps; strap extenders; exterior front, back, sides, and bottom; pockets; and accents.

2. Fuse the Thermolam Plus pieces to the wrong side of the corresponding pieces for the lining front, back, and sides.

3. Center a piece of Décor Bond on the wrong side of each accent rectangle and the exterior bottom, and fuse in place.

Shape the Side Panels

1. Measure and mark the upper edge of one exterior side 1½" from each corner. Draw a diagonal line from the left mark to the lower-left corner. Repeat on the right side. Cut along each line and discard the small triangles. ①

2. Align a drinking glass or other round object with the lower-left corner and trace around the curve. Trim along the line to round the corner. Round the lower-right corner in the same way.

3. Repeat steps 1–3 to shape the second exterior side and both lining sides.

Make the Pleated Panels

1. Draw a horizontal line 3½" below the 18" upper edge on the wrong side of the exterior front. Draw vertical lines, spaced as shown, from the upper edge of the exterior to the horizontal line. ②

2. Fold the fabric, right sides together, so the A lines meet. Pin the fold, making sure the entire lengths of the lines match. Sew along the A lines from the bag's upper edge to the horizontal line, backstitching to secure. ③

3. From the wrong side, flatten the pleat and press it open, centering the fabric over the seam.

4. Working from the right side, topstitch ⅛" from the seam on both sides, sewing for 3" from the upper edge. Backstitch to secure the pleats. ④

5. Repeat steps 2–4 for lines B, C, D, and E.

6. Repeat steps 1–5 to pleat the exterior back.

Make the Pockets

All seam allowances are ½" unless otherwise noted.

1. Fold one pocket in half, right sides together, to make a 7" x 6" rectangle. Sew along the three raw edges, leaving a 3" opening along one edge for turning.

2. Trim the corners diagonally to reduce bulk. Turn the pocket right side out and press. Topstitch ¼" from the folded edge of the pocket.

①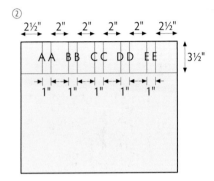

1½"

②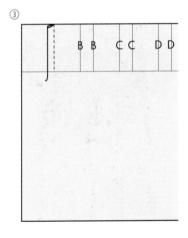

2½" 2" 2" 2" 2" 2½"

AA BB CC DD EE   3½"

1" 1" 1" 1" 1"

③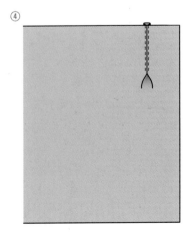

BB CC DD

④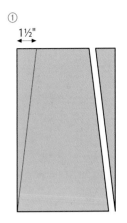

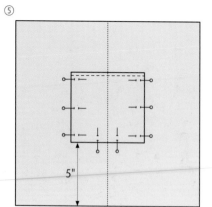

3. With the topstitched edge as the top of the pocket, finger-press the pocket in half to mark the vertical center. Do the same for the lining front. Place the pocket on the lining front, right sides up, with the pocket's lower edge 5" above the lower raw edge of the lining front and the centers aligned. Pin in place. ⑤

4. Edgestitch the pocket to the lining 1/8" from the sides and lower edge.

5. Repeat steps 1–4 to make a second pocket and attach it to the lining back.

Assemble the Lining

1. Attach the magnetic snap to the lining front and back, referring to "Magnetic Snaps" on page 16. The snap should be centered 1½" below the upper edges of the lining pieces.

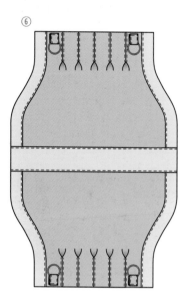

2. Sew the lining front to the lining back, right sides together, along the bottom edge, leaving a 6" opening at the center of the seam for turning. Press the seam allowances open.

3. Pin the assembled unit to one lining side, right sides together, matching the upper edges and easing the fabric to fit around the curves. Sew the pieces together. Clip the seam allowances, being careful not to cut into the stitches. Press. Attach the second lining side in the same way.

Make It Ease-y

I recommend sewing from the upper edge along both sides first and leaving the bottom of the side panel until last. This technique makes easing the fabric around the curves simpler, for even fabric distribution.

Make the Straps

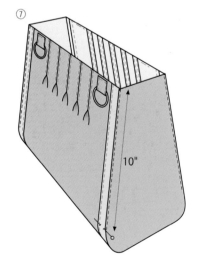

1. Press one strap extender in half, wrong sides together, to make a 2" x 2¼" rectangle. Open the crease and fold the edges in to meet at the center crease; press again. Refold along the original crease, enclosing the raw edges, and press once more to make a 2¼" strip of double-fold tape. Edgestitch 1/8" from each long edge. Make four.

2. Repeat step 1 to press a strap rectangle. Before edgestitching, open the strap and press ½" to the wrong side on both short ends. Refold and press to enclose all the raw edges. Edgestitch 1/8" from all four edges. Make two.

3. Slide a metal ring to the center of each strap extender. Fold the strap extender around the ring, matching the raw edges. Make four.

4. With a removable marker, mark the upper edge of the exterior front 1" from each side edge. Position a folded strap extender just inside each mark, matching the extender's raw edges to the upper raw edge of the exterior front. Baste ¼" from the raw edges.

5. Repeat step 4 to baste the remaining strap extenders to the exterior back.

Assemble the Exterior

1. Sew an accent piece to each side of the exterior front and exterior back. Press the seam allowances toward the accent fabric. Edgestitch the accents ⅛" from the seam line.

2. With right sides together, sew the assembled front to the assembled back along the lower edge. Press the seam allowances open.

3. Press ½" to the wrong side along each long edge of the exterior bottom. Place the bottom on the assembled bag, right sides up, centering it over the bottom seam. Edgestitch ⅛" from both long edges to attach the bottom to the bag. ⑥

4. Pin the assembled unit to one exterior side, right sides together, matching the upper edges and easing the fabric to fit around the curves. Sew the pieces together. Clip the seam allowances along the curves, being careful not to cut into the stitches. Press. Attach the second exterior side in the same way. Turn the bag right side out.

5. Fold the bag along one side seam line, wrong sides together. Place a pin 10" below the upper edge of the bag. Edgestitch through all layers ⅛" from the seam line, sewing from the upper edge to the pin. Repeat three times to stitch each accent panel where it meets the exterior side. ⑦

Finish the Bag

1. Slip the exterior into the lining, right sides together. Pin in place, matching the side seams, with the strap extenders tucked between the bag layers. Stitch the entire upper edge.

2. Turn the bag right side out through the opening in the lining. Press the seam allowances to the wrong side along the opening and either topstitch the opening closed by machine or slip-stitch it by hand. Press the bag well for a nicely finished look.

3. Edgestitch ⅛" from the upper edge.

4. Loop one strap end through the metal ring attached to a strap extender and knot the end of the strap to the ring. Conceal the short end of the strap inside the knot if desired. Knot the other end of the same strap to the second metal ring on the same side of the bag. Repeat to tie the second strap to the other side of the bag.

Two color variations of the Sound Check Bag

RESOURCES

Here's a list of my favorite sources and shopping sites for bag-making supplies.

Interfacing

Pellon: www.pellonprojects.com
Visit for information on all the interfacings Pellon manufactures, plus a whole library of free projects created by the Pellon Projects artists (including me!). Pellon interfacing is available at your local fabric or quilt shop.

Purse Hardware

Bag Purse Frames on Etsy: www.etsy.com/people/bagpurseframes
This shop in China stocks any purse hardware imaginable, including the twist lock I use in my Go-Go Bag.

Tall Poppy Craft Products: www.tallpoppycraft.com
This site, based in both New York and Australia, stocks hardware, purse handles, and much more.

Thread

Aurifil: www.aurifil.com
This company's wonderful thread, made in Italy, is available online and at your local quilt shop. Sturdy bags need the strongest thread. I use 40-weight thread for my bags.

Fabric

Pink Castle Fabrics: www.pinkcastlefabrics.com

Fabricworm: www.fabricworm.com

Fat Quarter Shop: www.fatquartershop.com

Free Spirit Fabrics: www.freespiritfabric.com

Kokka of Japan: www.sevenislandsfabric.com

Michael Miller Fabrics: www.michaelmillerfabrics.com

Riley Blake Fabric: www.rileyblakedesigns.com

Robert Kaufman Fabrics: www.robertkaufman.com

ACKNOWLEDGMENTS

This book would not be possible without the unwavering support of my family: my husband, Danny; my children, William and Violet; my parents; his parents; Oma and Opa; and in fact my entire family. They put up with my constant daydreaming and the need to be near a computer or sewing machine every single day. Also, I thank my best friend Kim for always thinking that I was the most talented person ever and making me almost believe it.

I'd also like to thank everyone who has ever read and enjoyed my blog. What began as a simple online journal of my sewing projects has become much more than I ever imagined it could be. Your comments and support on a daily basis mean so much to me, and I'm so lucky to count so many of you as my dear friends.

Thanks to my pattern testers for the book, who turned out some beautiful examples of my projects: Rebekah Bills, Katy Cameron, Jill Dorsey, Kelley Gilbert, Deedrie LaFolette, Allegory Lanham, Emily Lang, Caitlin McIntyre, Kristen Schubach, Melissa Shafer, Bree Wernimont, my mom, and especially Kim Munoz, who has made nearly every bag pattern I've ever put out. Thanks also to Elizabeth Dackson and Lindsay Conner for getting me to jump in and go for it.

I am so thankful to have Kay Whitt of Serendipity Studio as a friend and mentor. She has helped me more than I can ever say, and is always telling me to relax (the best advice!).

To Karen Burns, Karen Soltys, Rebecca Kemp Brent, and everyone who had a hand at turning out the final product that is this book: thank you for turning my daydreams into something beautiful that will hopefully inspire people to sew even more.

I am so thankful to Laurie Wisbrun, Thomas Knauer, Sheri McCulley, and Tula Pink for sending me their fabrics to turn into bags. Your confidence means so much to me! Thank you Jennifer Paganelli for your help and support! Thank you to Jina from Riley Blake Fabrics, Nancy from Free Spirit Fabrics, and Christine from Michael Miller Fabrics for providing me with beautiful fabrics to work with for the bags.

I owe a lot to Erin (who has become such a great friend), Cris, and Alexandra at Pellon for really helping me get off the ground with creating bag patterns. I honestly didn't know that I could do it until I tried, and since then there's been no looking back. It is so wonderful working with first-rate interfacing and batting.

And to you, reader, for picking up this book . . . I hope you like what you see, and that it inspires you to sew something pretty for yourself. Where sewing is concerned, never be afraid to try new things, and sew as much as you can!

ABOUT THE AUTHOR

My name is Sara Lawson, and I am a wife and mother living in Chicago. I began my sewing blog, Sew Sweetness (www.SewSweetness.com), in September of 2010. As it grew, I found myself finishing several projects a week so that I could showcase them on my blog, and I looked forward so much to all the comments from my lovely readers. In December of 2011, I started writing free sewing patterns for Pellon via the company's Pellon Projects website. Several of my bag patterns have been published in sewing and quilting magazines, and I taught classes at Sewing Summit 2012. I love creating, and I always have several bag, clothing, or quilt projects on a mental list, waiting to be sewn! Visit me online to find great downloadable sewing patterns.